# The Squire Tarantella for Cello

# Practice Edition

A Learn Cello Practically Book

Written and Compiled by Cassia Harvey
*Tarantella* by W. H. Squire
Duet by Myanna Harvey, based on W. H. Squire

CHP428

©2022 C. Harvey Publications®
All Rights Reserved.
www.charveypublications.com - print books
www.learnstrings.com - downloadable books
www.harveystringarrangements.com - chamber music

## Table of Contents

| Section | Page |
|---|---|
| What's In the Book | 5 |
| How to Practice Using This Edition | 6 |
| Understanding Symbols and Terms | 7 |
| Reading and Playing Half and Whole Steps | 8 |
| Preparing to Play the Tarantella | 9 |
| Reading Treble Clef in the Tarantella | 10 |
| Using Thumb Position in the Tarantella | 11 |
| Spiccato | 12 |
| Bowing Style in the Tarantella | 13 |
| Preparatory Exercises for the Tarantella | 14 |
| Tarantella - With Study Notes | 56 |
| Tarantella - Complete Piece | 65 |
| Tarantella - Cello Duet | 68 |
| Tarantella - Cello II Part for Performance | 75 |
| Tarantella - Piano Accompaniment | 78 |
| Cello Curriculum Segments - Where to Place the Tarantella | 84 |

# What's In the Book

### How to Practice Using This Edition
These pages have ideas for developing a practice strategy to learn the *Tarantella*. From explanations of symbols and terms to a description of half and whole steps, these pages tell you how the book can be most helpful to you.

### Preparatory Exercises
The most difficult parts in the *Tarantella* were identified and then broken down and taught in these pages. The Preparatory Exercises for each section are followed by the *Tarantella with Study Notes*.

### Tarantella With Study Notes
The entire *Tarantella* has been written with notes for study, including marked positions, some beat marks, and extension reminders.

### Complete Piece
The cello part to the *Tarantella* is here, for practice or performance.

### Tarantella with Cello Duet Part
The entire *Tarantella* is included with a cello duet part that will allow you to practice or perform the piece with your teacher or with another cellist. If you'd like to perform the duet, the Cello II part is included by itself, after the score, so page turns can be easier.

### Piano Accompaniment
The piano accompaniment is included for study, practice, or performance.

### Cello Curriculum Segment - Where to Place the Tarantella
These pages show how the *Tarantella* can fit in a cello curriculum, along with recommended methods, etudes, and supplemental study books.

©2022 C. Harvey Publications®  All Rights Reserved.

## How to Practice Using This Edition

1. Play and master the **Preparatory Exercises**. First, learn the exercises slowly. Then, when you are more comfortable with the notes, play the exercises closer to the actual tempo of the **Tarantella**.

2. You may also, at the same time, practice the piece using the **Tarantella with Study Notes** that follows the **Preparatory Exercises**.

3. Once you have learned the piece fairly well, transition to the **Complete Piece** section (page 65.)

4. Play the **Tarantella with Cello Duet** part with your teacher or with another cellist.

5. If you know a pianist, play with the included **Piano Accompaniment**.

6. See what to play next in a typical **Cello Curriculum**, using the lists at the end of the book (page 84.)

## Play-Along Sound Files

Some Play-Along Sound Files for this book may be found at https://soundcloud.com/charveypublications/sets/squiretarantella

The files are listed according to their page in the book.

Soundcloud can be accessed on your computer or on your mobile device, via their free app.

©2022 C. Harvey Publications® All Rights Reserved.

# Understanding Symbols and Terms

In this book, **Roman Numerals** indicate strings (never positions.)
I = A string, II = D string, III = G string, IV = C string

**Beat marks** are notated by small notes above the regular notes that indicate how to subdivide for counting.

**Positions** are indicated by numbers and words: 4th position, 3rd position, etc.

> *Extend* refers to reaching two whole steps with the fingers of the left hand. For more explanation of extensions, see a method such as **Cello Stretching: Extended First Position** (CHP243.) Occasionally, an arrow will be used to remind you to extend forward or backward.
> *Closed* refers to a regular position where the hand is not extending.

**Metronome markings** are included in the **Tarantella with Study Notes** for both study and performance tempos. They are listed as a range (i.e. from 76-100.) When you have learned the notes and bowings fairly well, you might want to start playing with the metronome. You can start slowly, with the metronome beat equaling an eighth note and as you progress, set the metronome to equal a dotted quarter note. Continue getting faster until you reach the performance tempo where you feel most comfortable.

These markings are only approximate; feel free to play the piece at a slower or faster tempo!

**Study tempo:** ♪=144-160 and then ♩.=76-100

**Performance tempo:** ♩.=104-144

**Two separate fingerings** are included for measures 64 and 204. In this case, pick the fingering that you prefer. You may also choose your own fingerings and bowings that are not included.

©2022 C. Harvey Publications® All Rights Reserved.

# Reading and Playing Half and Whole Steps

Here are some practical ways to think of steps on the cello:
- The space between each finger in the regular (closed) lower positions is a half step.
- The space between three fingers (for instance 1st finger and 3rd finger) in regular (closed) lower positions is a whole step.
- To reach a whole step with 1st and 2nd fingers, you must extend or stretch. In this case, the thumb should move up under 2nd finger to allow you to reach easily.
- As you move up through the positions, the spaces between the notes get smaller. A half step in first position will be much bigger than a half step in seventh position.
- In the higher positions, both whole and half steps can be played by any two adjacent fingers (for instance 2nd and 3rd finger). Think of the half steps as "small spaces" and the whole steps as "big spaces" to help differentiate between the two.

**Half steps are marked this way:**

Half step space

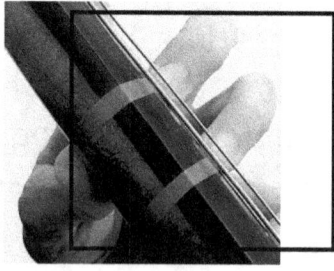

**Whole steps are marked this way:**

Whole step space with 1st and 3rd finger (closed postion.)

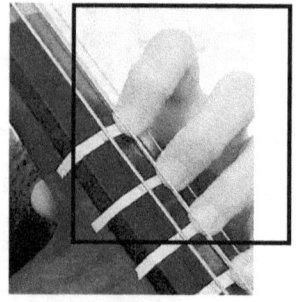

Whole step space with 1st and 2nd finger (extended position.)

# Preparing to Play the Tarantella

## Prerequisite Skills

- Ability to read and play in 6/8 timing.
- Ability to read, shift to, and play in second, third, and fourth position.
- Ability to play fairly long slurs (two measures or more) in 6/8 timing.
- Have some familiarity with fifth position and understanding of shifting into the higher positions.
- Ability to play a three-octave D major scale (see *Learning Three-Octave Scales on the Cello*; CHP356, pages 16-19.)

## Recommended Books to Study Before Playing the Tarantella

- *The Triplet Book for Cello, Part One* (CHP233) and *Part Two* (CHP259) for left and right hand agility in 6/8 timing.
- *Fourth Position for the Cello* (CHP131) or *Fourth Position Study Method* (CHPD078)
- *Second Position for the Cello* (CHP114)
- *Third Position for the Cello* (CHP116)
- The first 8 pages in *Fifth Position for the Cello* (CHP198)
- The first 12 pages of exercises in *Learning Three-Octave Scales on the Cello* (CHP356)

## Reading Treble Clef in the Tarantella

The Tarantella has a few notes in treble clef. In cello music, we see treble clef used in the higher positions, often when the thumb is being used. The notes below show one way bass clef intersects with treble clef. In many ways, treble clef is just an extension or continuation of bass clef.

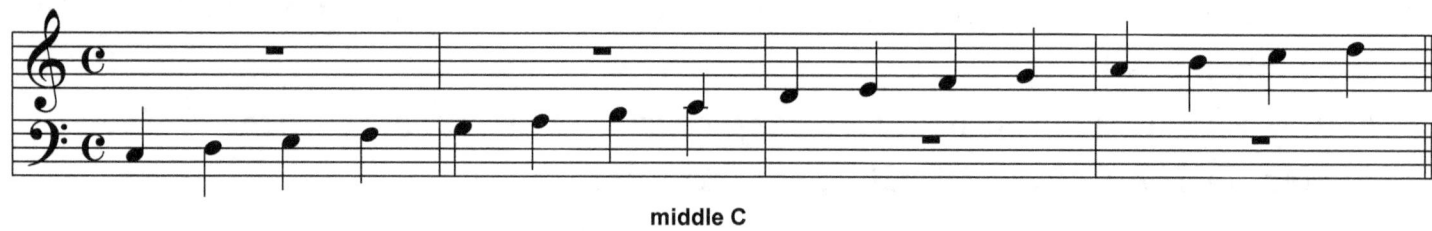
middle C

Here is a note chart showing some cello notes in bass clef and how they are written in treble clef.

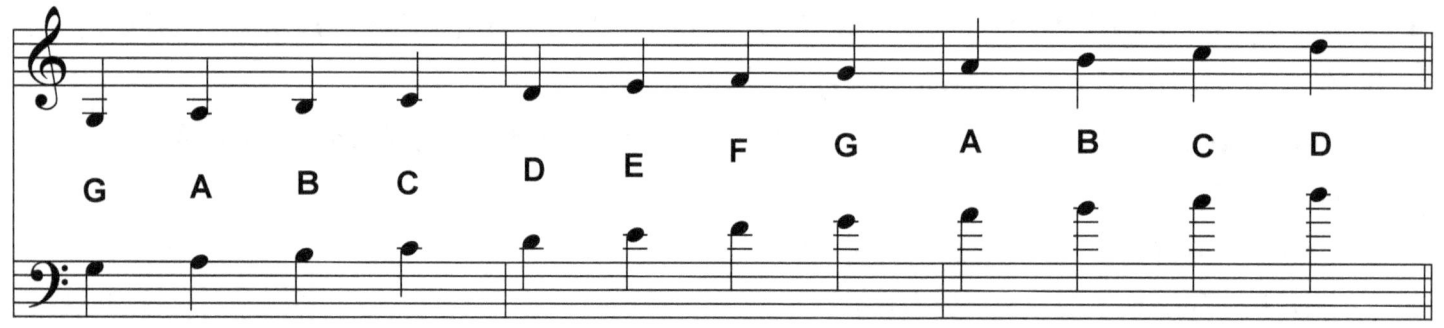

And here are the notes from the Tarantella (measures 62-64 and 203-205) written in treble clef and also in bass clef. You can see why Squire used treble clef to make the notes more readable, without as many ledger lines as bass clef uses.

©2022 C. Harvey Publications® All Rights Reserved.

## Using Thumb Position in the Tarantella

- Thumb Position does not refer to a place but to a hand position that includes the thumb. Thumb Position may be used anywhere on the cello. In the *Tarantella*, the thumb will be placed where the mid-string harmonic is, across two strings.
- Place the thumb on its side, across the A and D strings. The thumb touches the A string on the *side of the knuckle* and on the D string, depending on the length of your thumb, *nearer the top of the thumb, on the side of the nail*.
- Play on the tips of the remaining fingers (keep fingernails very short.)
- Keep the left wrist straight to support the hand and the thumb.
- Balance your hand over all the fingers and the thumb equally.

This is the sign for the thumb: ⟶ ♀

**Thumb Position in the Tarantella**

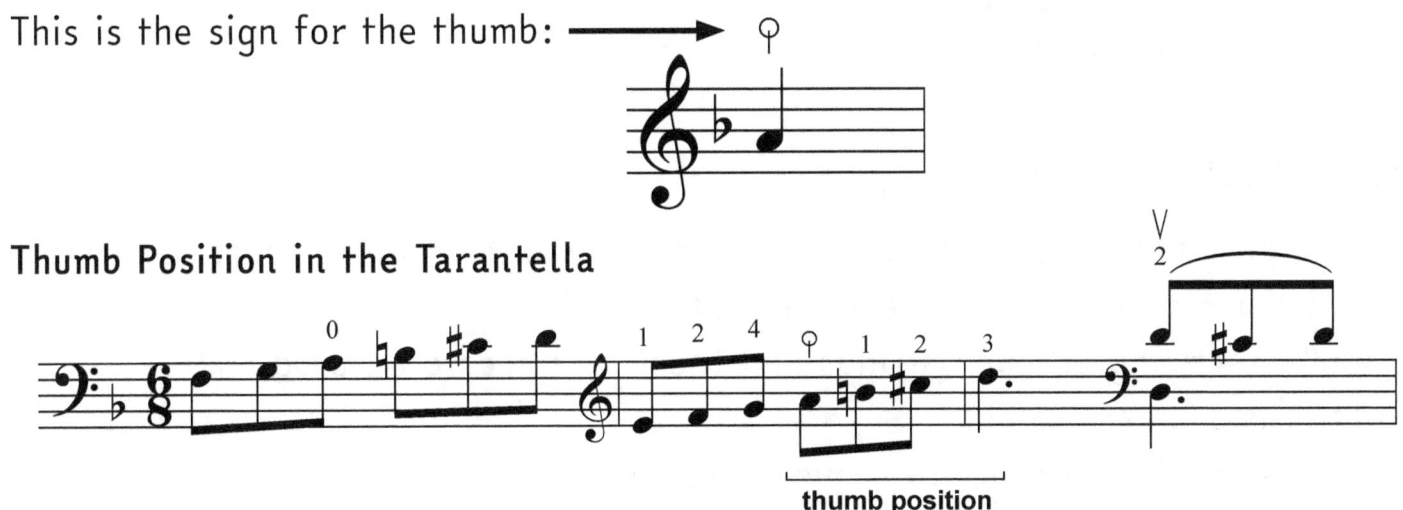

thumb position

©2022 C. Harvey Publications®  All Rights Reserved.

# Spiccato

## How Spiccato Works

Because both the bow hair and the string are flexibly stretched, the bow can bounce on the string. By relaxing your arm and hand and timing the bounce correctly, you can get a very good spiccato sound.

## Where to Play Spiccato

Bouncing is often easiest at the balance point of the bow, between where you hold the bow and the middle of the bow. This will vary from bow to bow.

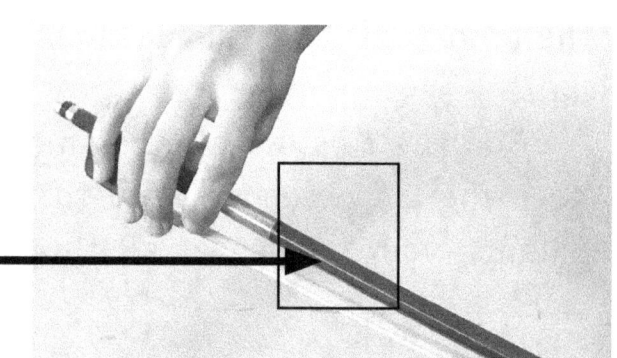

On the string, spiccato works best when played near the fingerboard (not near the bridge.)

### Spiccato in 6/8 timing:

Note: if the tempo is too slow, the bow will not bounce.

### Practice Starting Spiccato

## How to Practice Spiccato

- Since spiccato needs to be played at a fairly quick tempo in order to work, start learning spiccato on repeated notes.
- Start practicing on open strings and then try spiccato on predictable patterns such as scales.
- The Tarantella has spiccato in measures 93-96.

©2022 C. Harvey Publications®  All Rights Reserved.

## Bowing Style in the Tarantella

The Squire Tarantella is a light, quick, rhythmic piece. To help keep the music light, cellists often lift their bows between some of the slurs. Here is an example of where the bow might be lifted (commas indicate bow lifting):

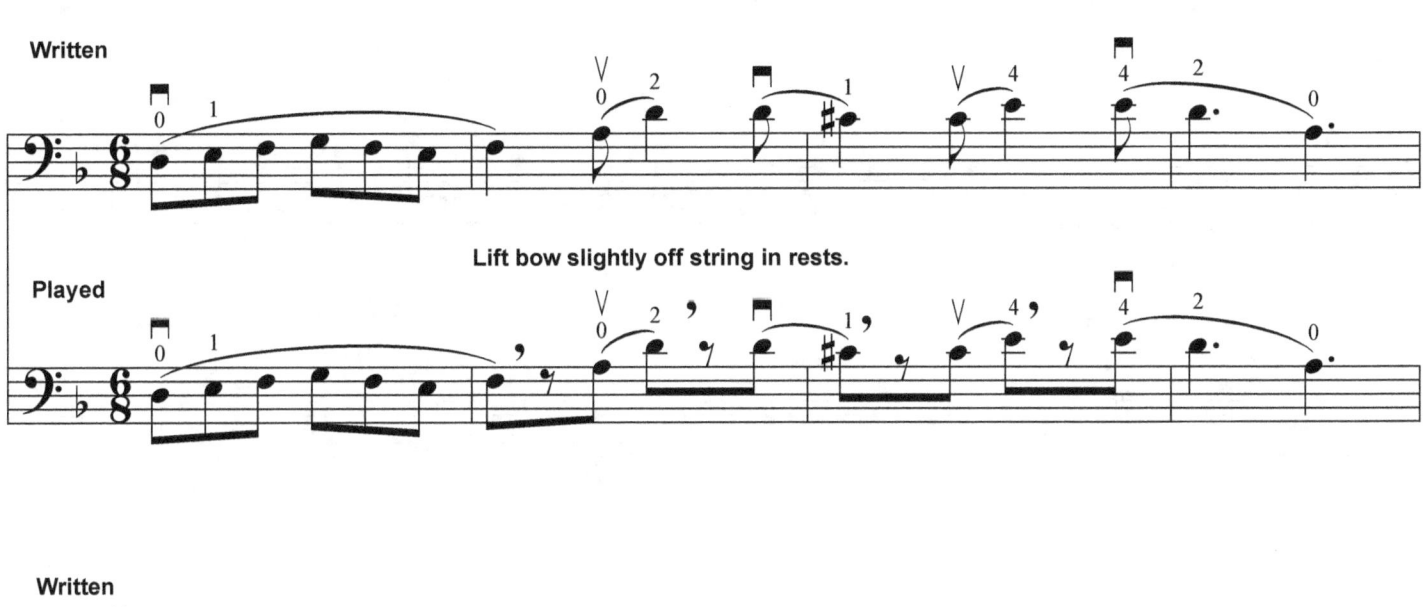

When lifting your bow, stay as close to the string as possible. The higher you lift your bow, the harder it will be to land it on the string! Staying close to the string when you lift will also help you stay in tempo and not slow down.
*Note:* Lifting the bow as indicated above generally only works when the Tarantella is being played at or close to concert tempo.

## 1. Warm-Up: Setting the Key
### Measures 1-72

### 3. Finger Agility
#### Measures 9-14

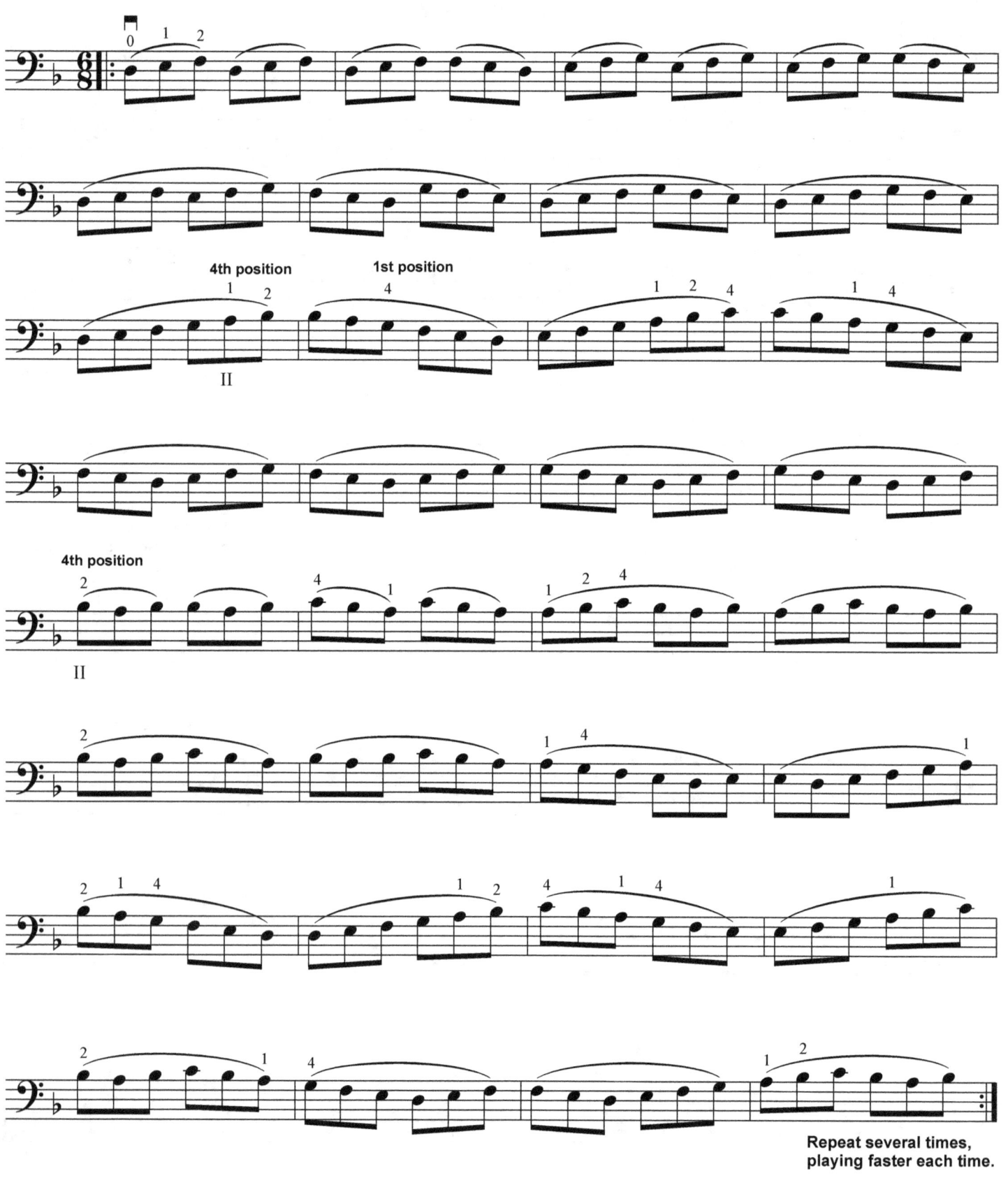

Repeat several times, playing faster each time.

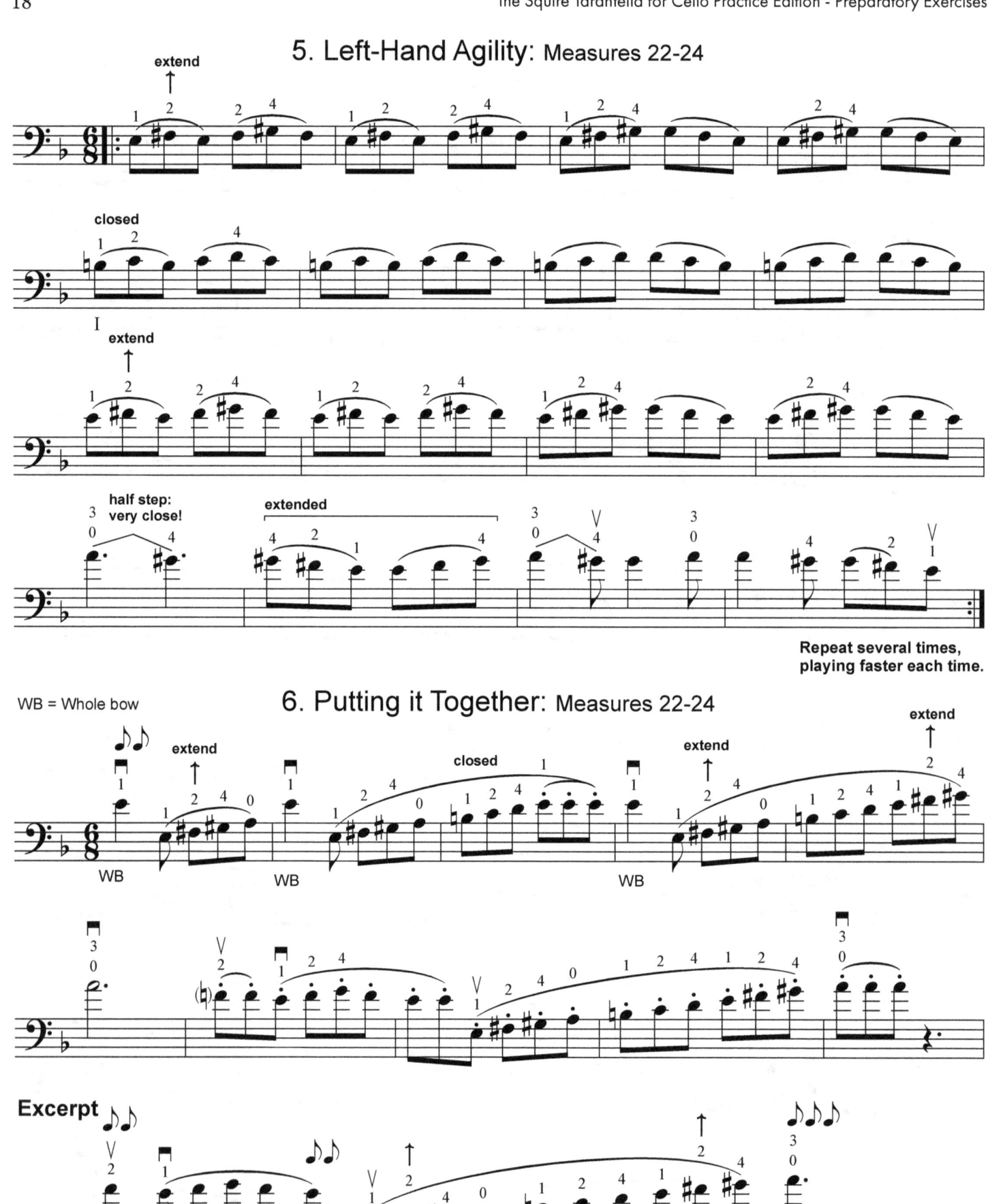

The Squire Tarantella for Cello Practice Edition - Preparatory Exercises

©2022 C. Harvey Publications®  All Rights Reserved.

The Squire Tarantella for Cello Practice Edition - Preparatory Exercises

## 12. Rhythmic Shifting II: Measures 24-32

**Excerpt**

Now, the previous measures are repeated exactly, but with an open D string played at the same time as the notes.

**Repeat several times, playing faster each time.**

©2022 C. Harvey Publications® All Rights Reserved.

## 13. Learning the Bowing: Measures 40-56

The Squire Tarantella for Cello Practice Edition - Preparatory Exercises
23

**Note:** If playing Fingering II, skip to page 32.

### 14. Learning the Notes: Measures 63-64, Fingering I

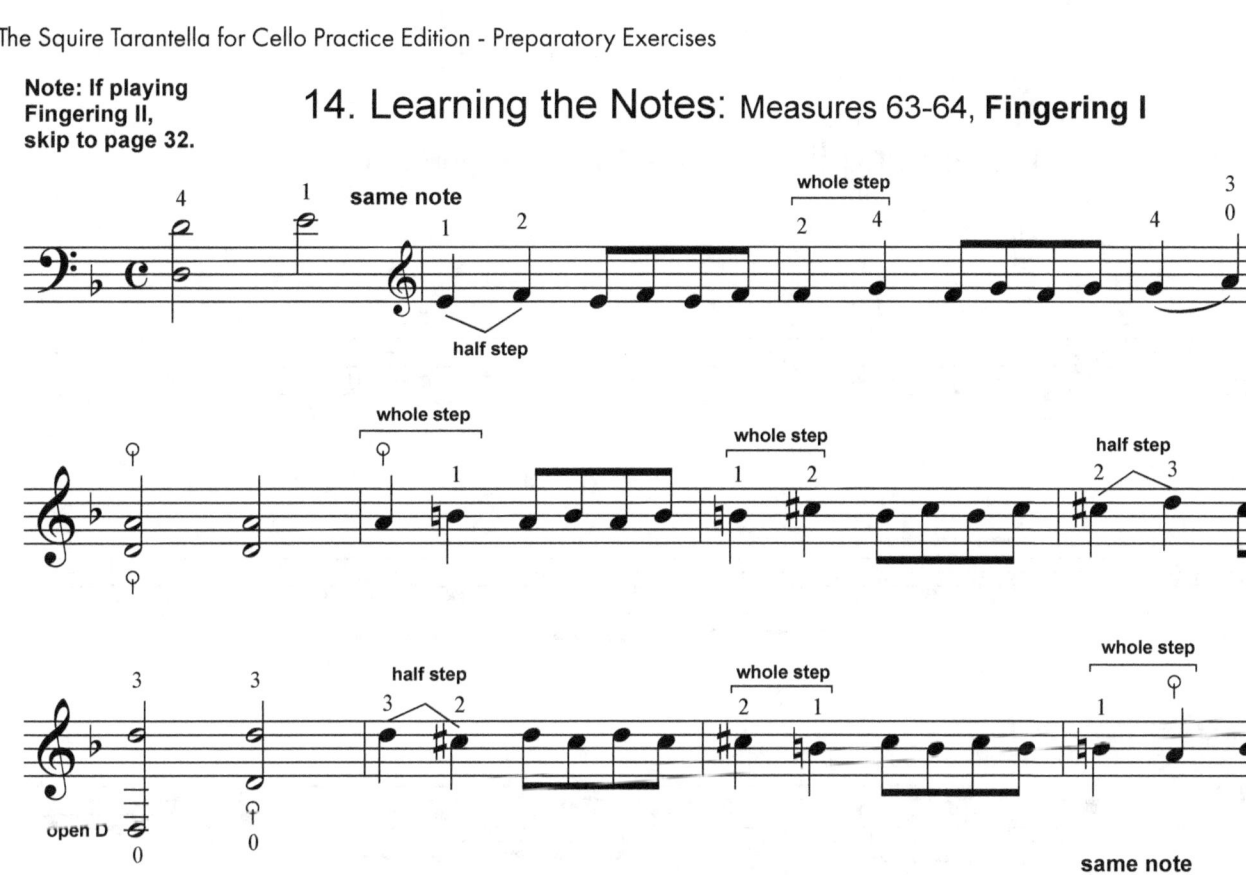

### 15. Shifting I: Measures 63-64, Fingering I

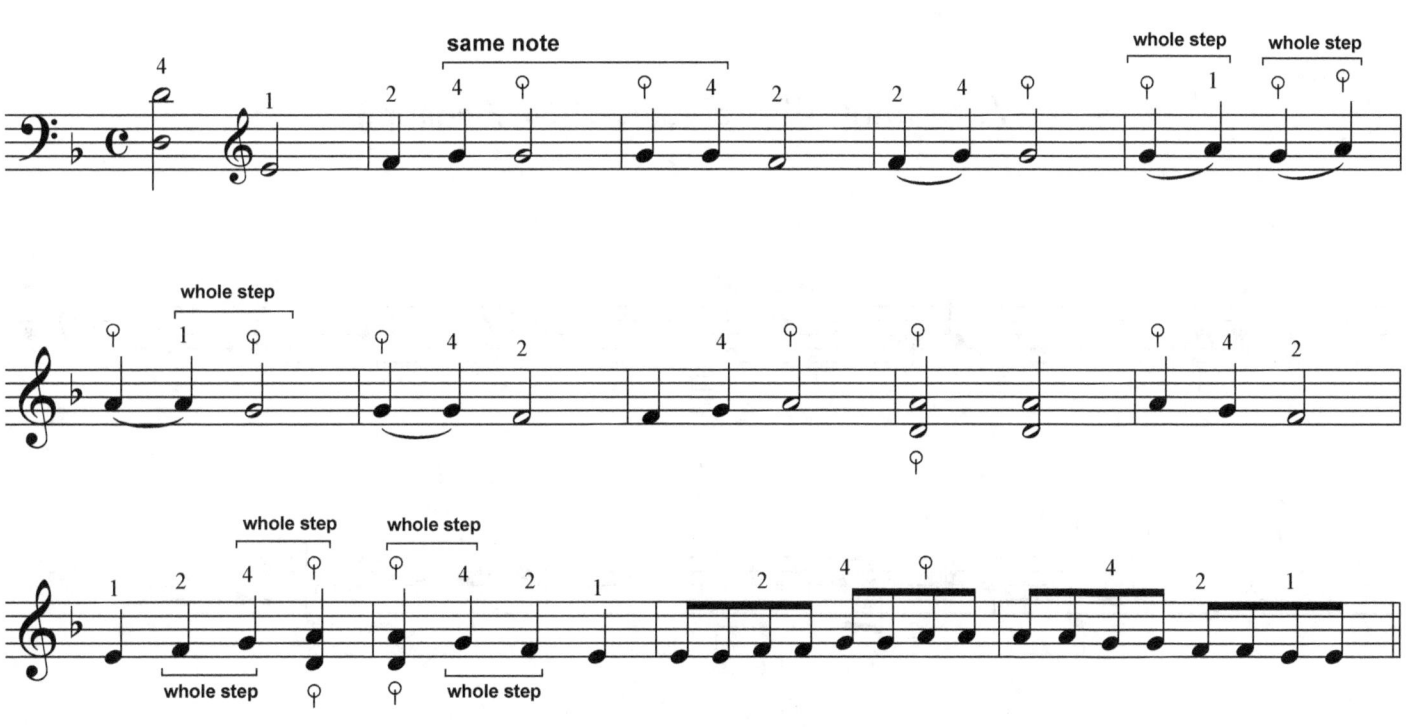

©2022 C. Harvey Publications® All Rights Reserved.

### 16. Shifting II: Measures 63-64, **Fingering I**

### 17. Shifting III: Measures 63-64, **Fingering I**

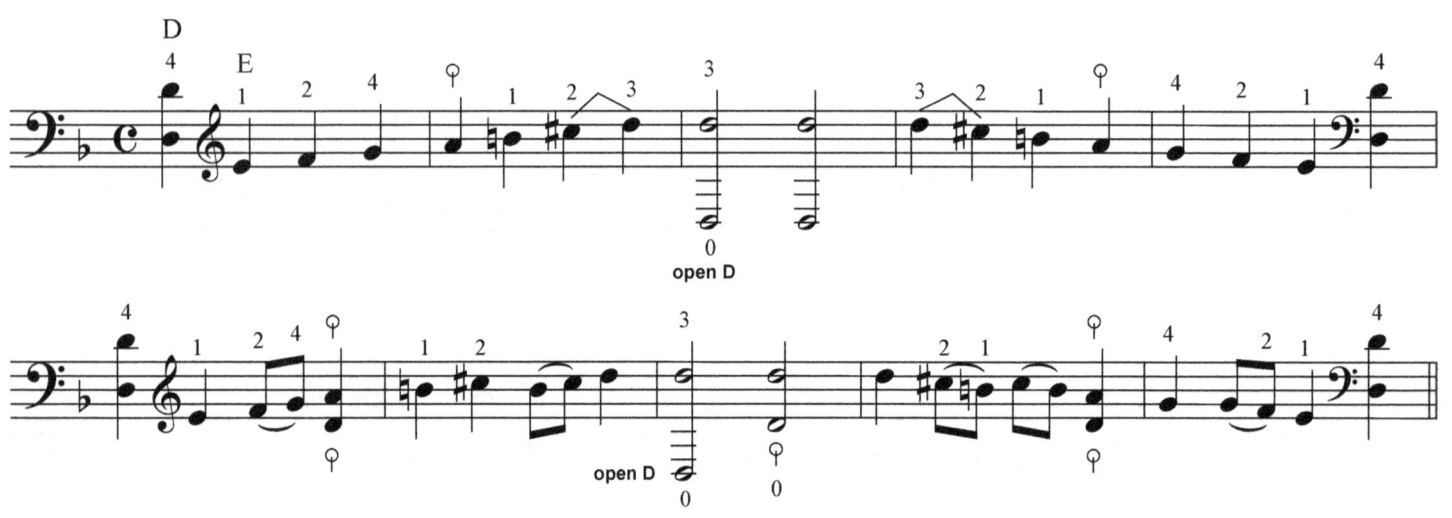

## 18. Shifting IV: Measures 63-64, **Fingering I**

### 19. Rhythmic Shifting for Speed I: Measures 63-64, **Fingering I**

The Squire Tarantella for Cello Practice Edition - Preparatory Exercises

## 20. Shifting in Triplets: Measures 63-64, Fingering I

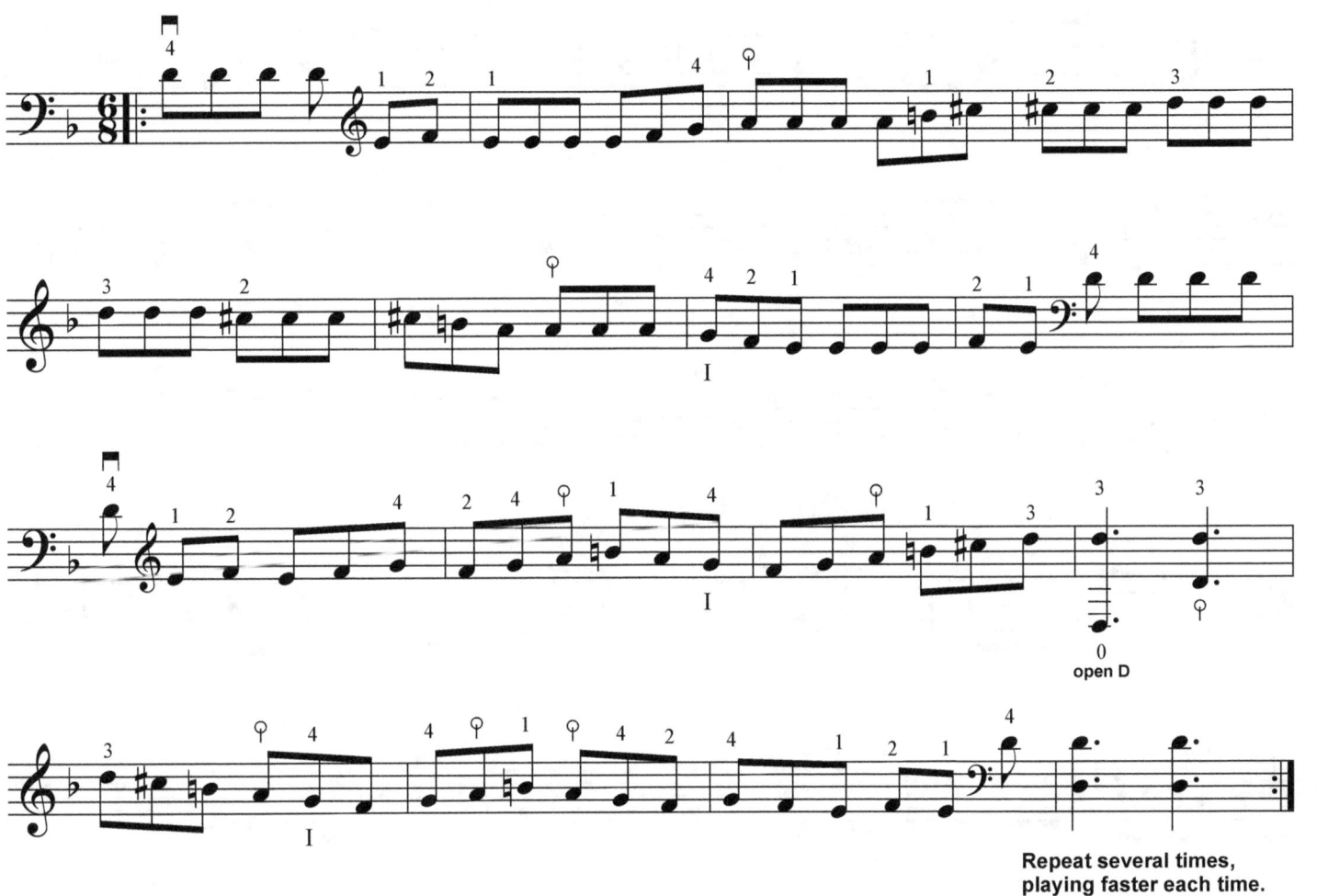

**Repeat several times, playing faster each time.**

## 21. Rhythmic Shifting for Speed II: Measures 63-64, Fingering I

**Repeat several times, playing faster each time.**

## 22. Rhythmic Shifting for Speed III: Measures 63-64, Fingering I

**Repeat each measure until it is as fast as possible.**

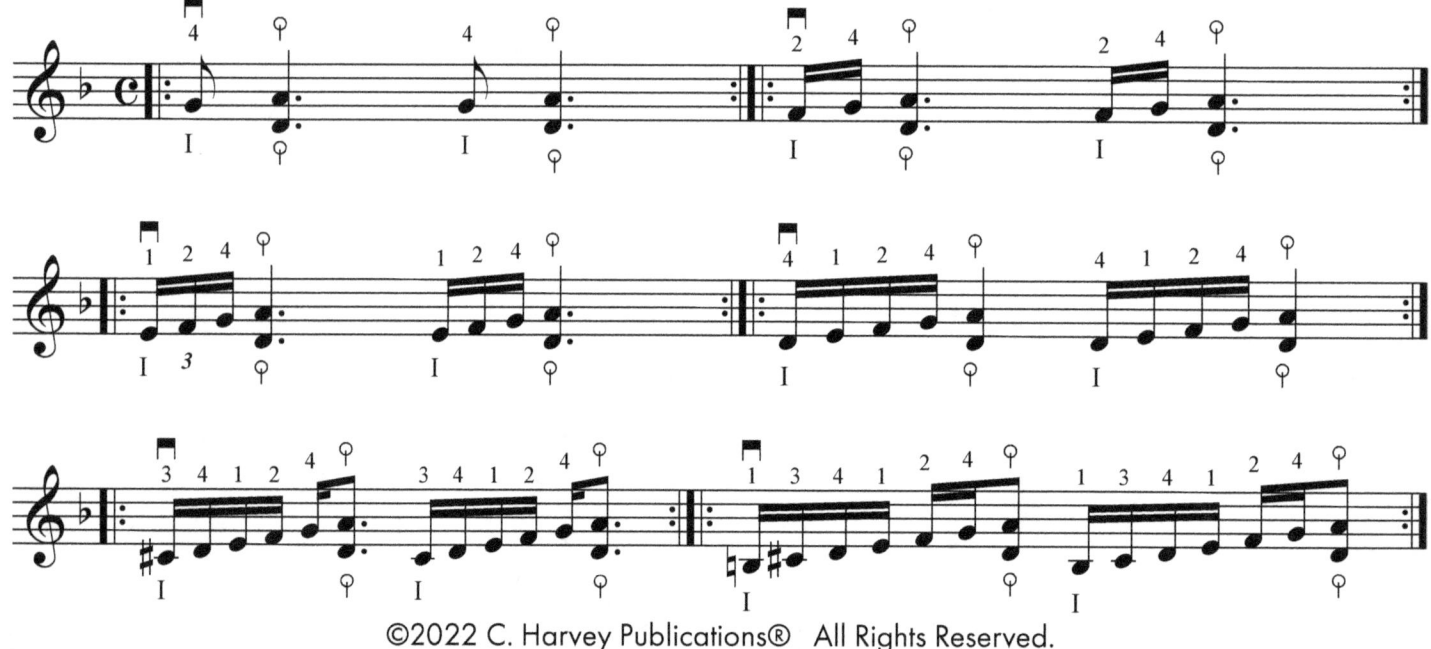

The Squire Tarantella for Cello Practice Edition - Preparatory Exercises

### 23. Rhythmic Shifting for Speed IV: Measures 63-64, **Fingering I**

same note

### 24. Rhythmic Shifting for Speed V: Measures 63-64, **Fingering I**

**Repeat this exercise several times, playing faster each time.**

### 25. Rhythmic Shifting for Speed VI: Measures 63-64, **Fingering I**

**Repeat this exercise several times, playing faster each time.**

©2022 C. Harvey Publications® All Rights Reserved.

## 26. Rhythmic Shifting for Speed VII: Measures 63-64, Fingering I

## 27. Shifting Quickly onto the Thumb I: Measures 63-64, Fingering I

The Squire Tarantella for Cello Practice Edition - Preparatory Exercises
31

### 28. Shifting Quickly onto the Thumb II: Measures 63-64, **Fingering I**

Repeat this line until it is as fast as possible.

### 29. Rhythmic Shifting for Speed VIII: Measures 63-64, **Fingering I**

same note

Note: If playing

©2022 C. Harvey Publications®  All Rights Reserved.

The Squire Tarantella for Cello Practice Edition - Preparatory Exercises 33

### 32. Shifting II: Measures 63-64, Fingering II

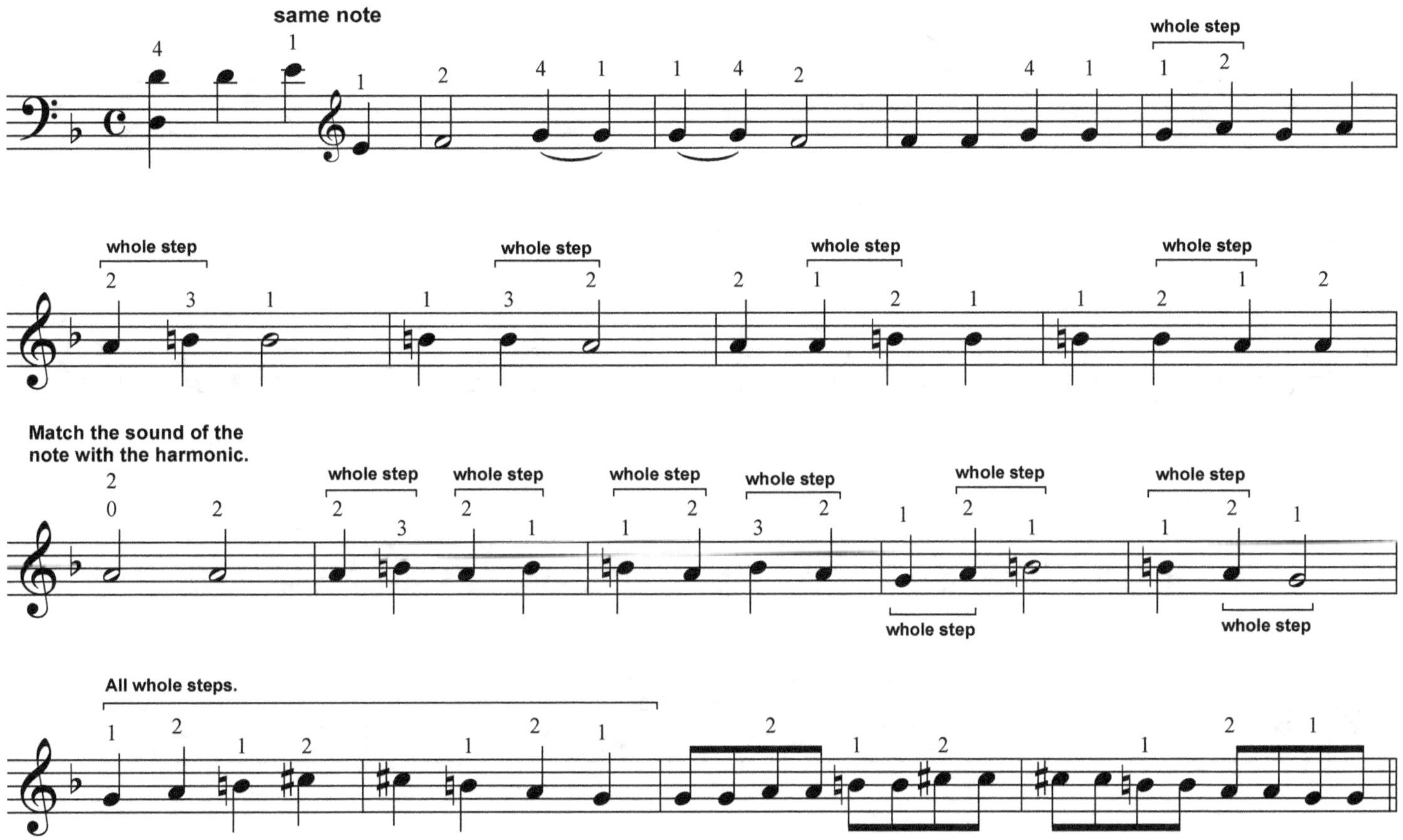

### 33. Shifting III: Measures 63-64, Fingering II

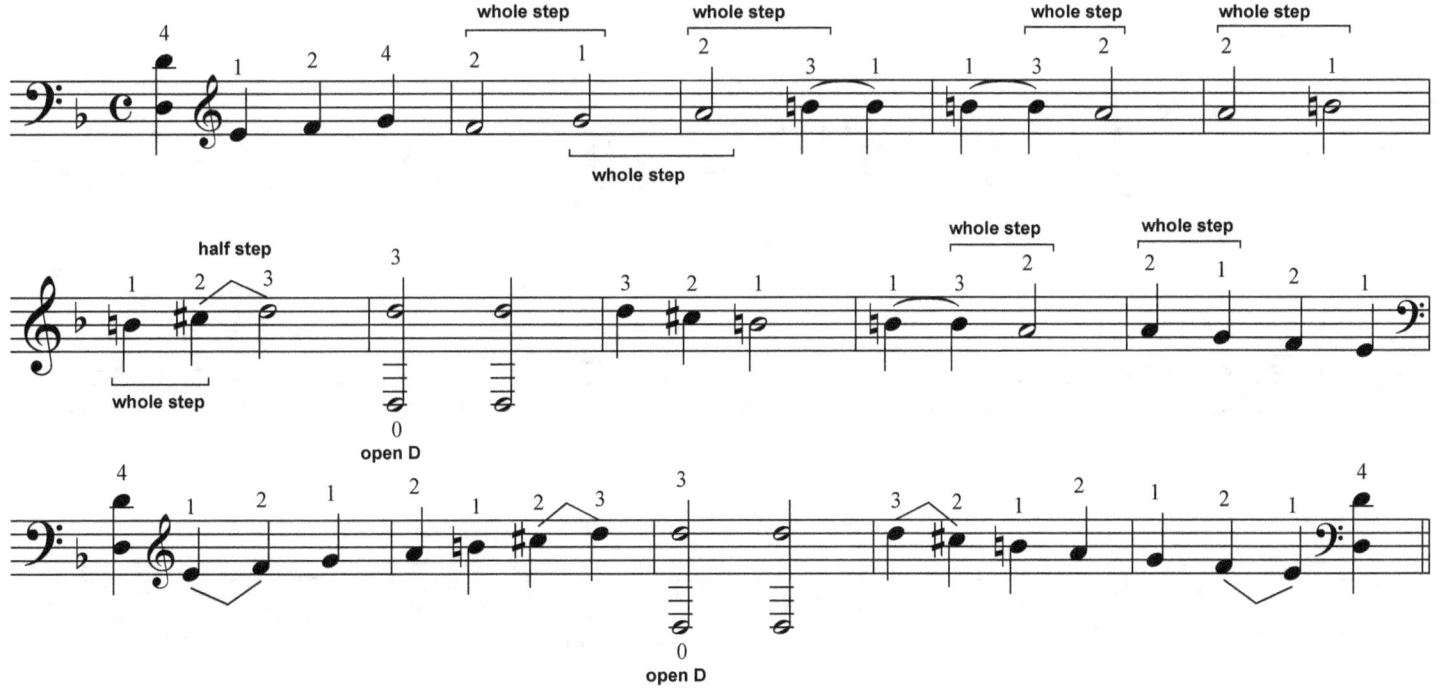

©2022 C. Harvey Publications® All Rights Reserved.

### 34. Shifting IV: Measures 63-64, Fingering II

### 35. Rhythmic Shifting for Speed I: Measures 63-64, Fingering II

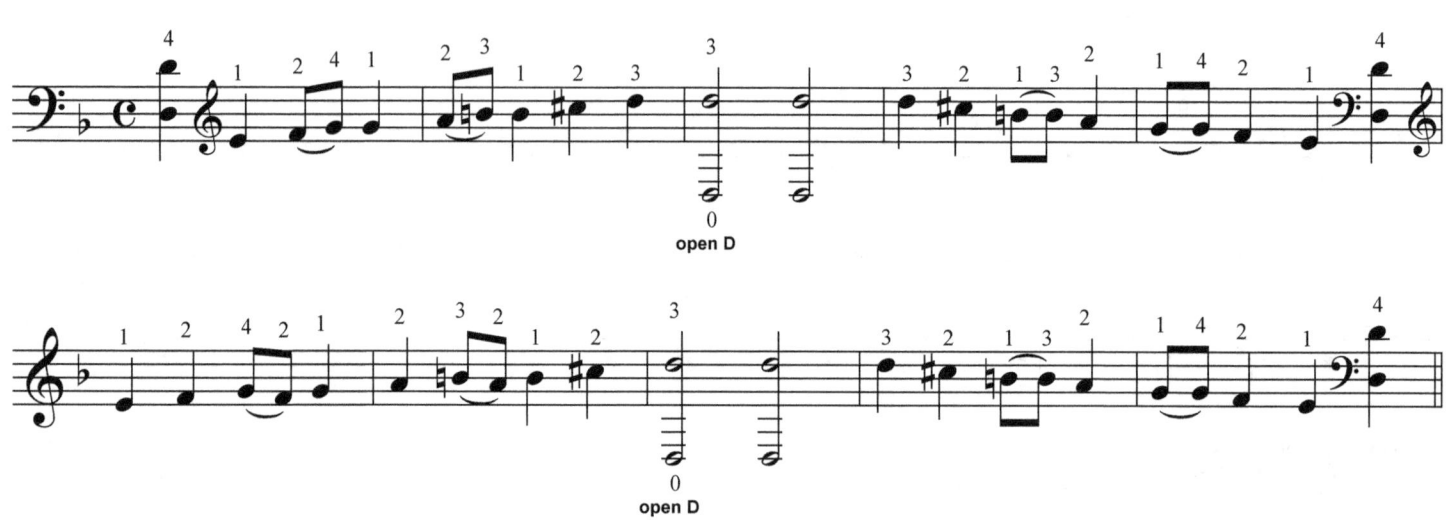

## 36. Shifting in Triplets: Measures 63-64, Fingering II

## 37. Rhythmic Shifting for Speed II: Measures 63-64, **Fingering II**

## 38. Rhythmic Shifting for Speed III: Measures 63-64, **Fingering II**

**Repeat several times, playing faster each time.**

©2022 C. Harvey Publications®  All Rights Reserved.

### 39. Rhythmic Shifting for Speed IV: Measures 63-64, **Fingering II**

same note

### 40. Rhythmic Shifting for Speed V: Measures 63-64, **Fingering II**

**Repeat this exercise several times, playing faster each time.**

### 41. Rhythmic Shifting for Speed VI: Measures 63-64, **Fingering II**

**Repeat this exercise several times, playing faster each time.**

©2022 C. Harvey Publications®  All Rights Reserved.

The Squire Tarantella for Cello Practice Edition - Preparatory Exercises

## 44. Learning the Notes: Measure 68

©2022 C. Harvey Publications®   All Rights Reserved.

## 45. Shifting I: Measure 68

The Squire Tarantella for Cello Practice Edition - Preparatory Exercises    41

## 46. Shifting II: Measures 68-72

©2022 C. Harvey Publications®   All Rights Reserved.

## 47. Shifting Forward and Backward: Measures 68-72

Repeat several times, playing faster each time.

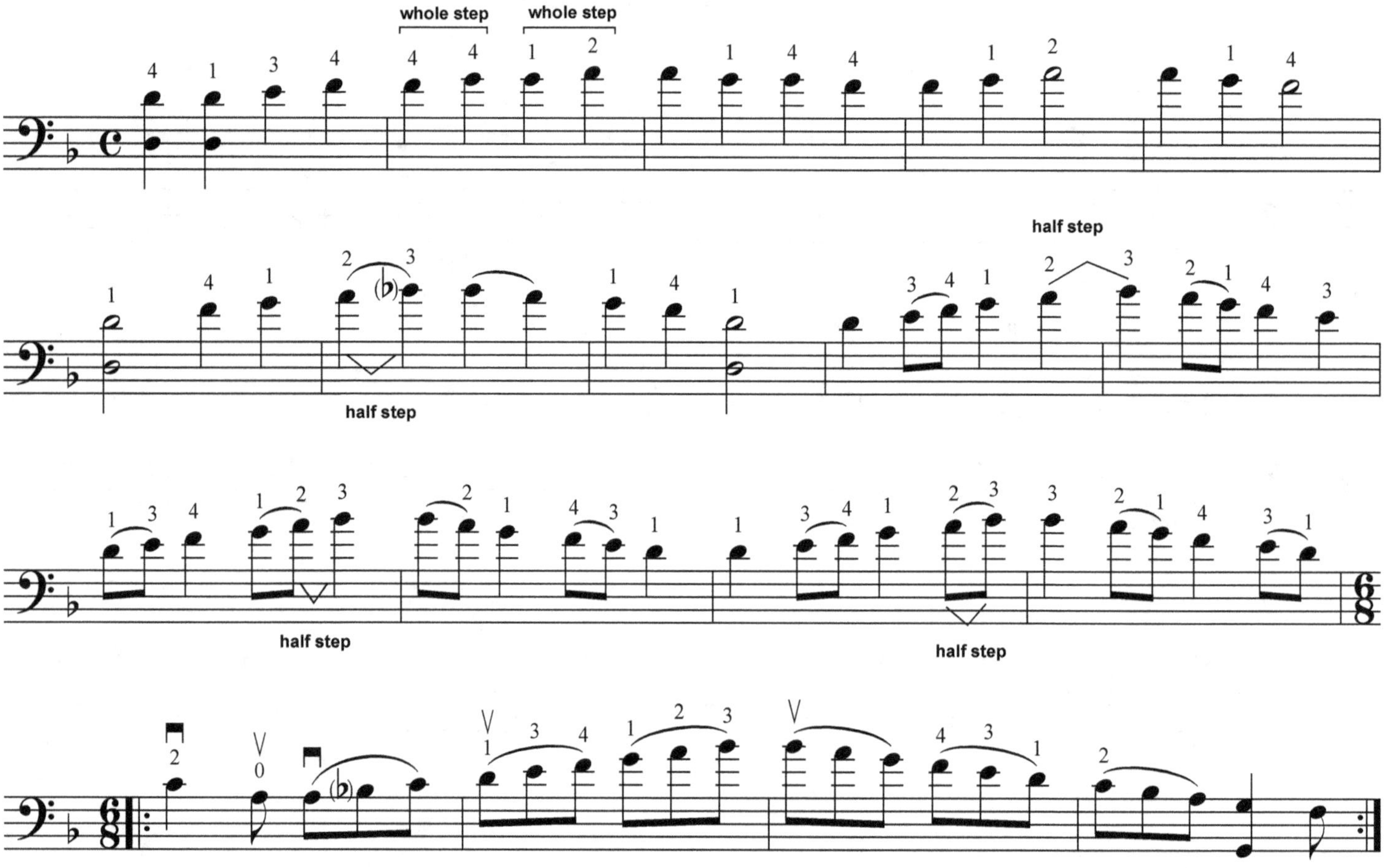

## 48. Focus on Shifting Backwards I: Measures 68-72

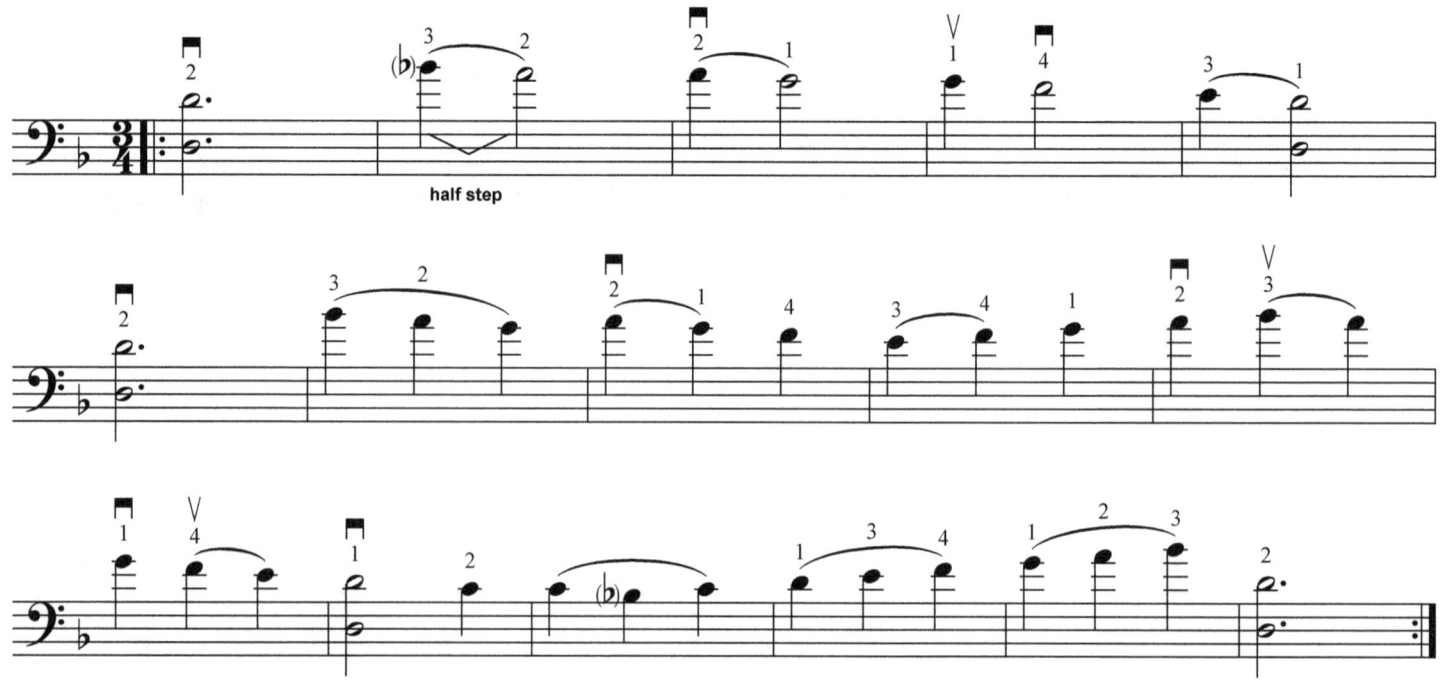

The Squire Tarantella for Cello Practice Edition - Preparatory Exercises

### 49. Focus on Shifting Backwards II: Measures 68-72

### 50. Chords: Measures 71-72

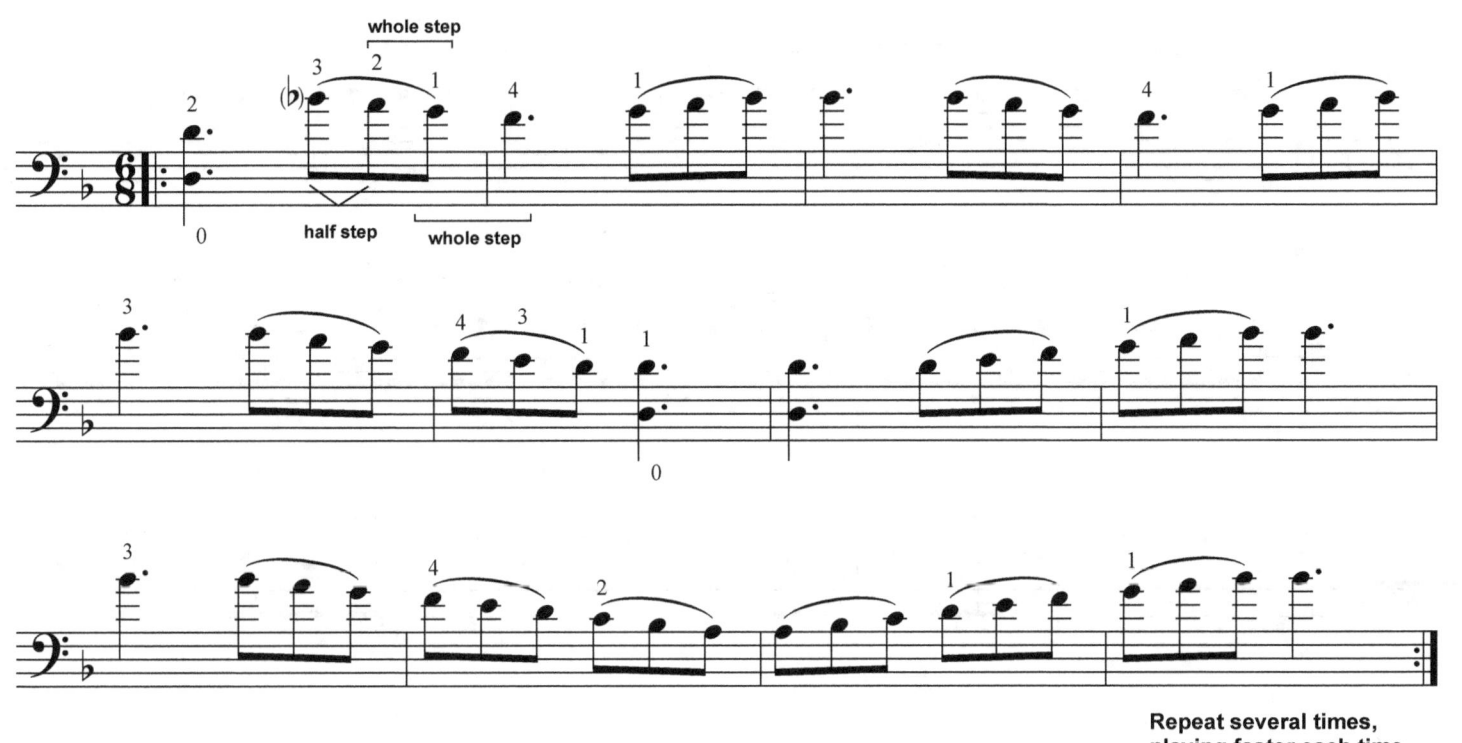

## 51. Rhythm: Measures 73-76

## 52. Learning the Notes: Measures 80-81

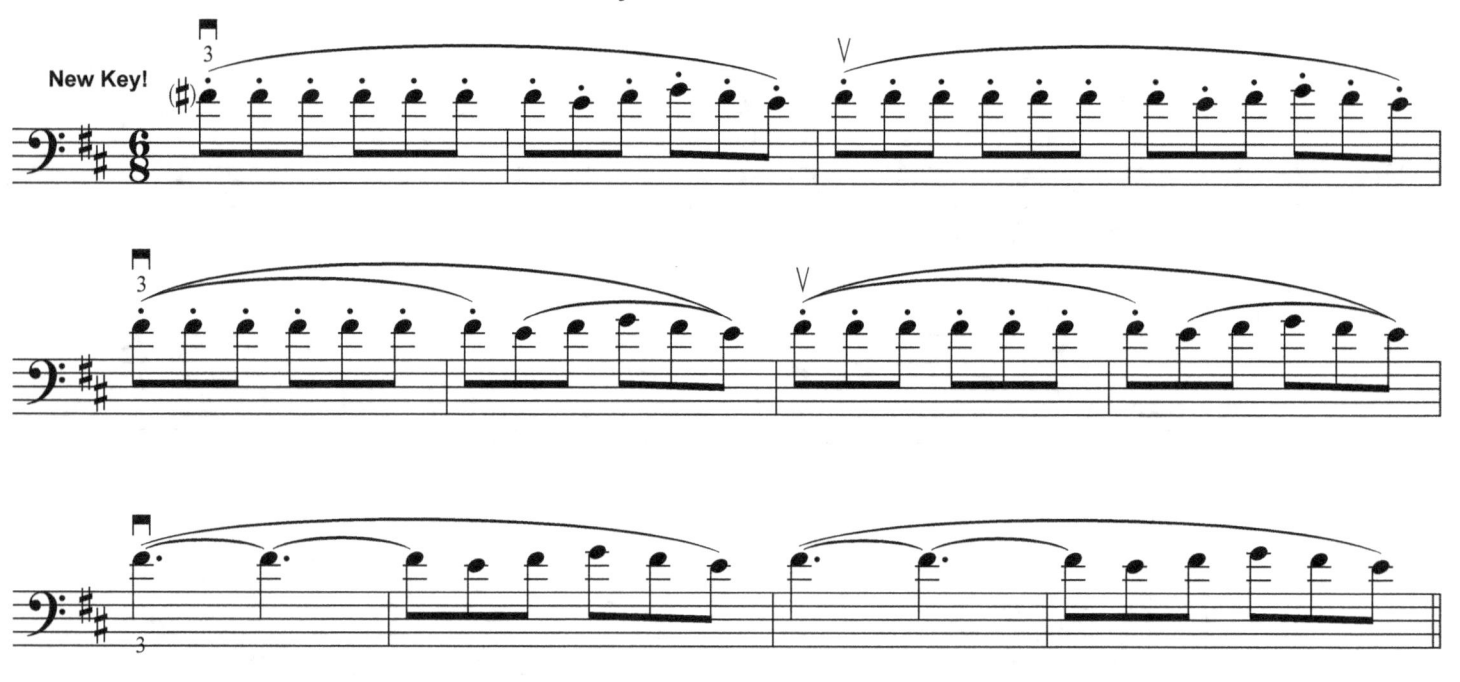

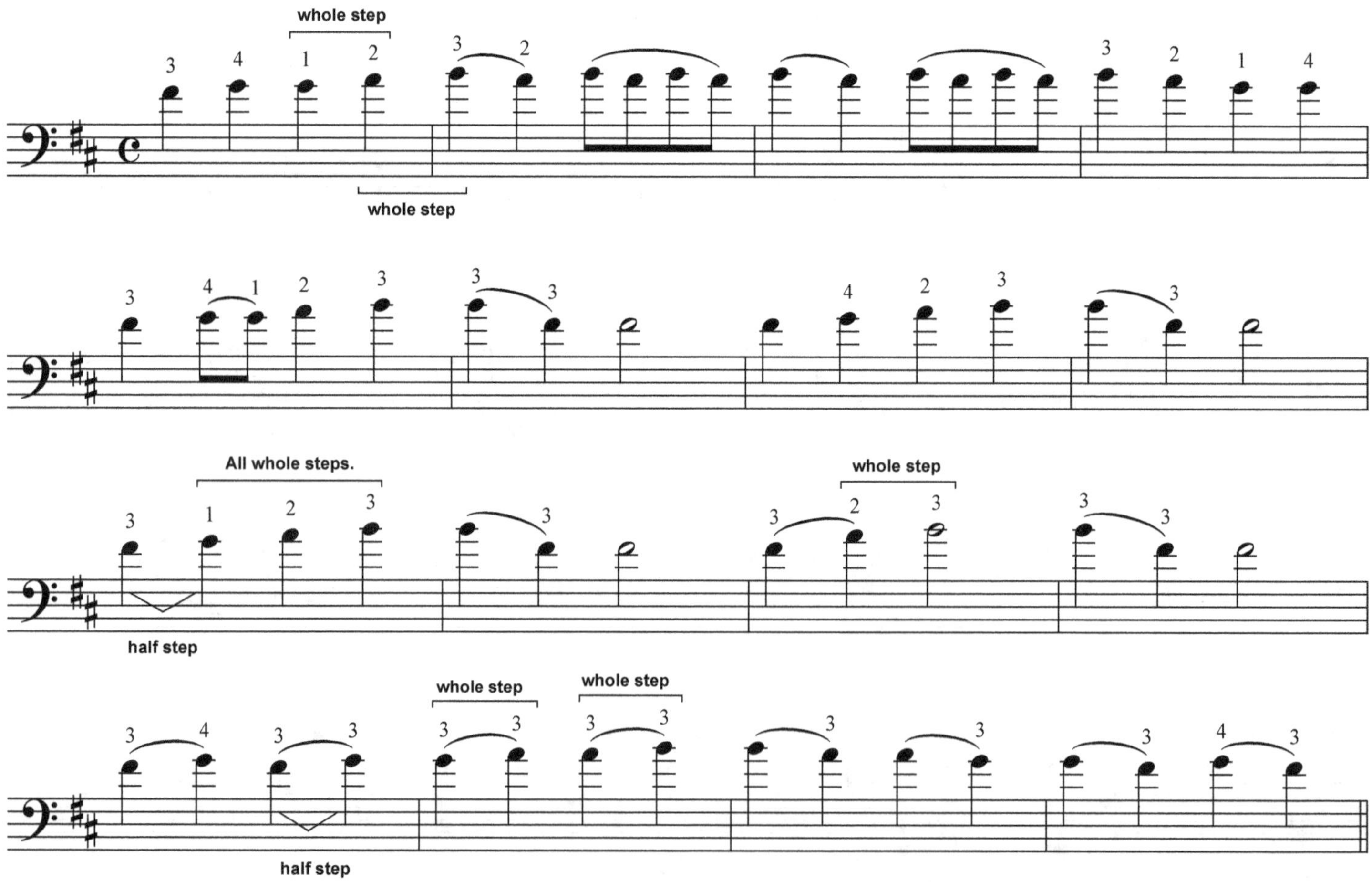

### 53. Shifting in 6/8: Measures 80-81

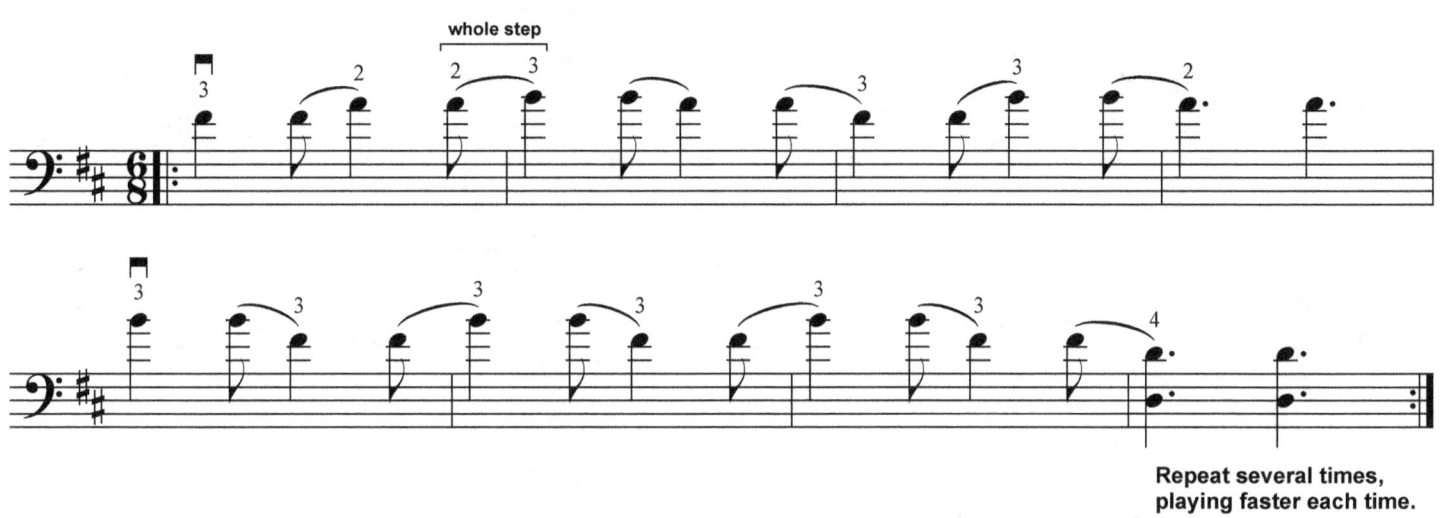

Repeat several times, playing faster each time.

### 54. Using 3rd Finger to Learn Distance: Measures 80-81

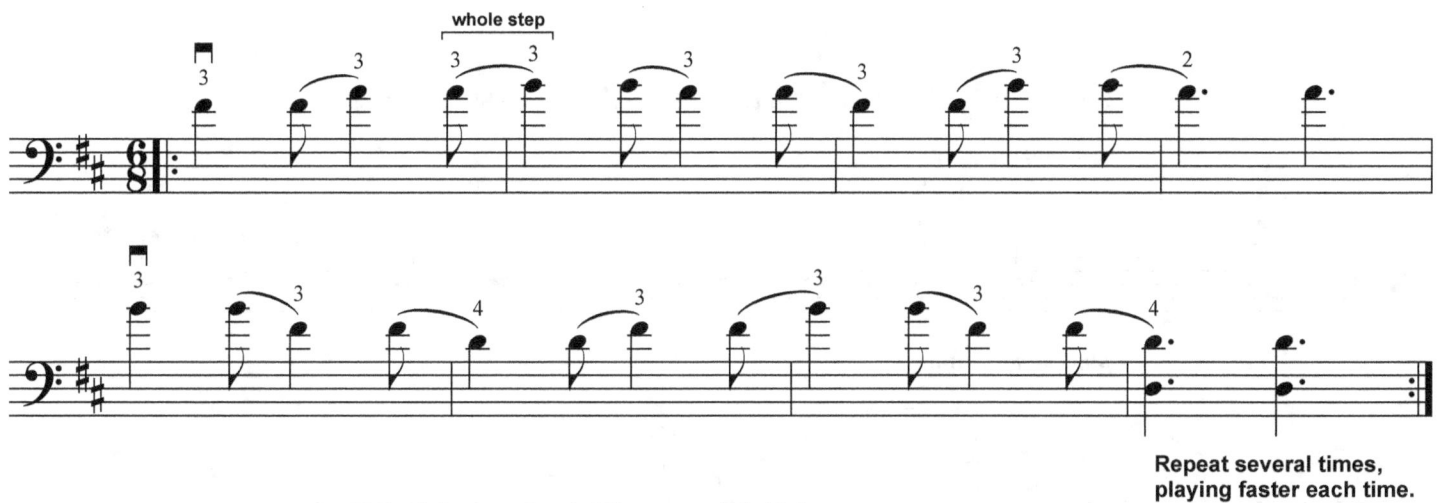

Repeat several times, playing faster each time.

### 55. More 3rd Finger Shifting: Measures 79-81

46

The Squire Tarantella for Cello Practice Edition - Preparatory Exercises

### 56. Rhythm: Measures 79-81

### 57. Shifting and Light Spiccato: Measures 95-98

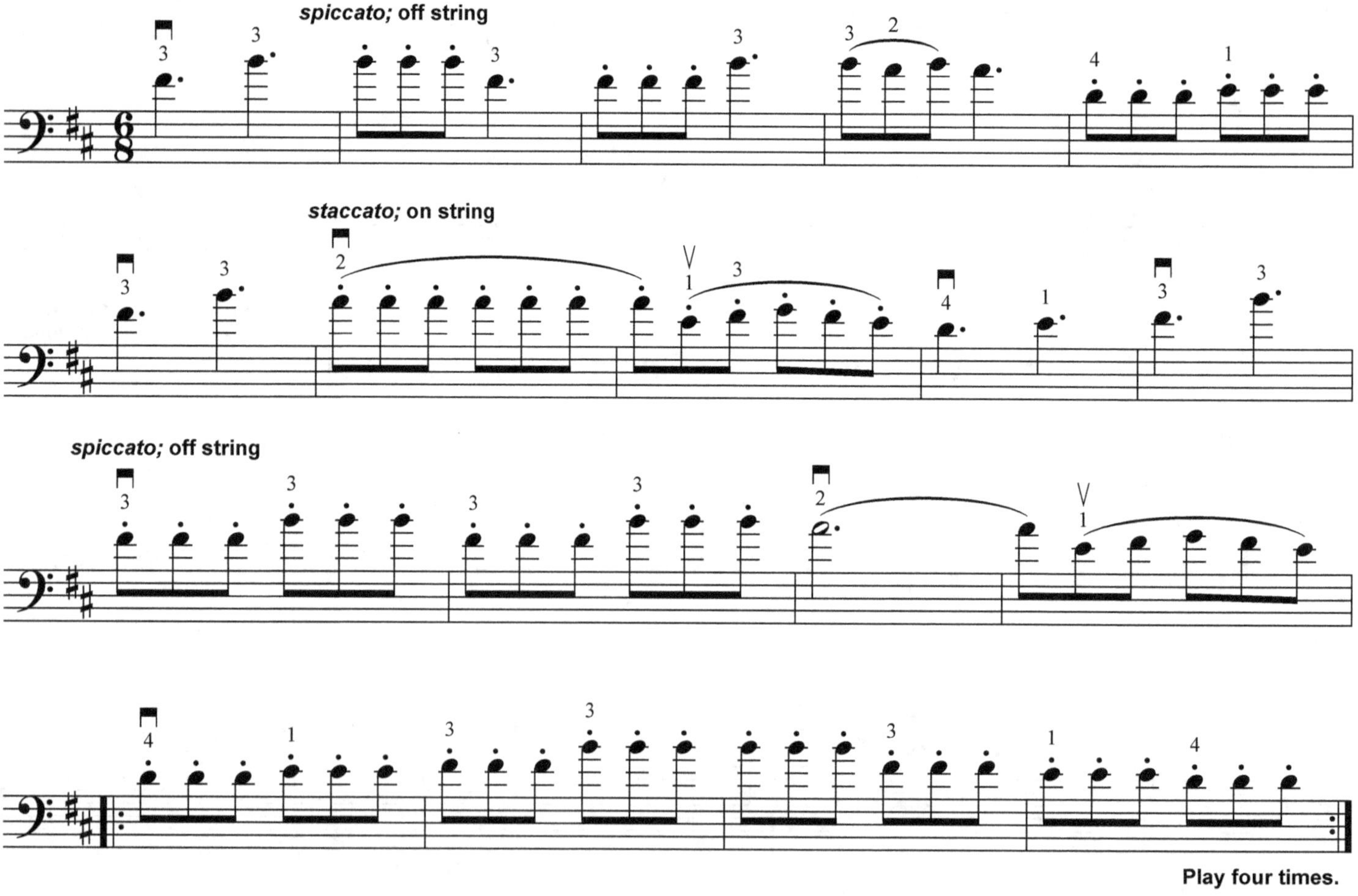

**Play four times.**

©2022 C. Harvey Publications®   All Rights Reserved.

The Squire Tarantella for Cello Practice Edition - Preparatory Exercises
47

### 58. Learning the Notes: Measures 101-106

### 59. Rhythm: Measures 104-108

©2022 C. Harvey Publications®  All Rights Reserved.

## 62. Learning the Fifth Position Notes: Measures 113-116

## 63. Shifting from Second to Third Position: Measures 146-147

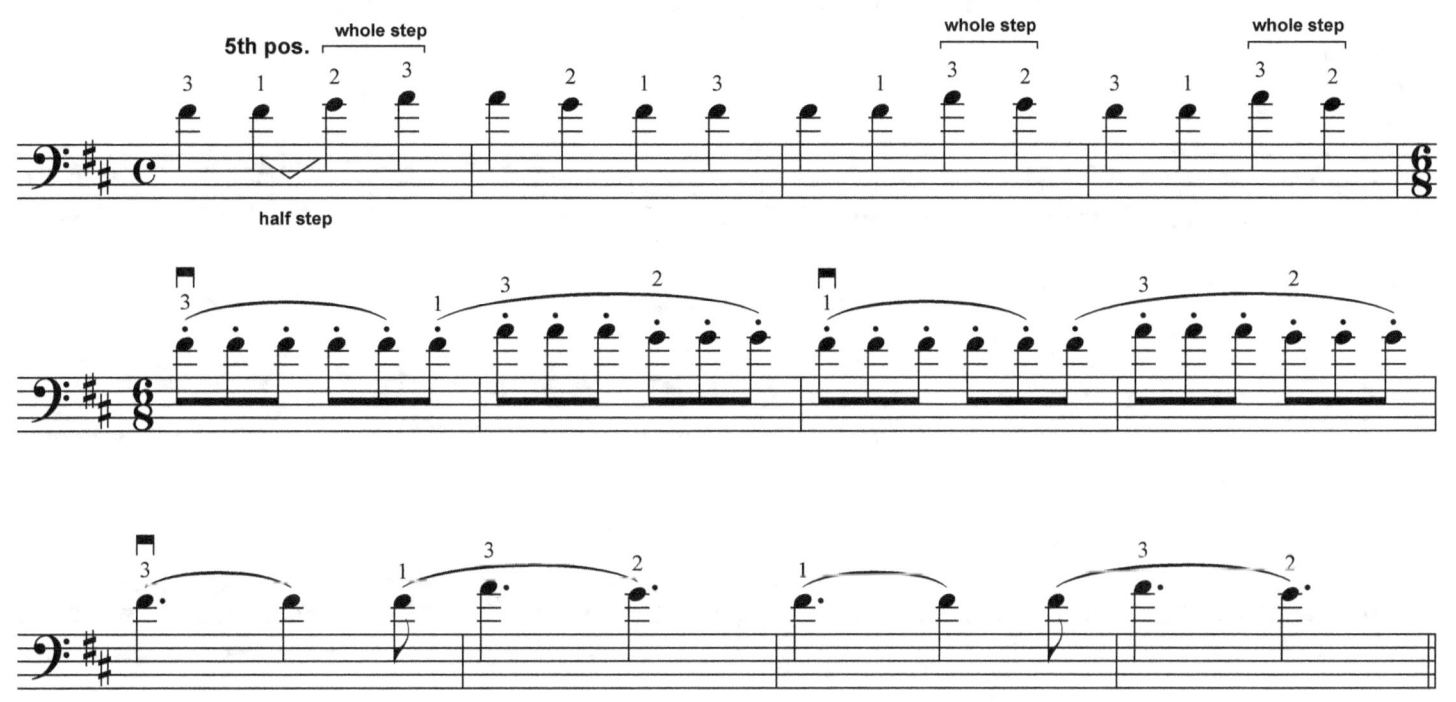

## 64. Shifting and Agility I: Measures 221-228

## 65. Shifting and Agility II: Measures 221-228

**If this is in tune, it may be repeated faster.**

### 66. Shifting and Agility III: Measures 221-228

### 67. Shifting and Agility IV: Measures 221-228

The Squire Tarantella for Cello Practice Edition - Preparatory Exercises
53

### 68. Speed I: Measures 221-228

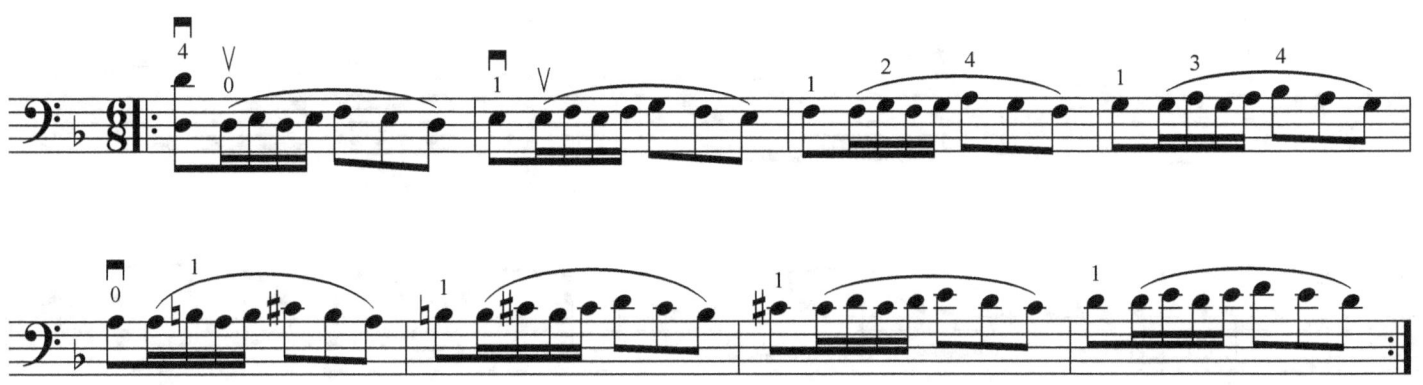

**Repeat several times, playing faster each time.**

### 69. Speed II: Measures 221-228

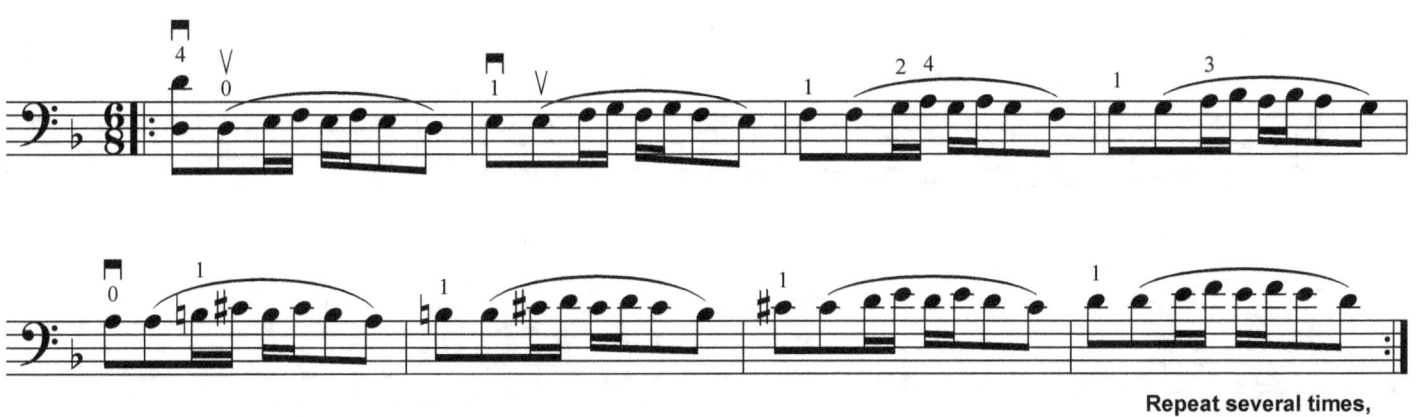

**Repeat several times, playing faster each time.**

### 70. Speed III: Measures 221-228

**Repeat several times, playing faster each time.**

©2022 C. Harvey Publications®  All Rights Reserved.

### 71. Speed IV: Measures 221-228

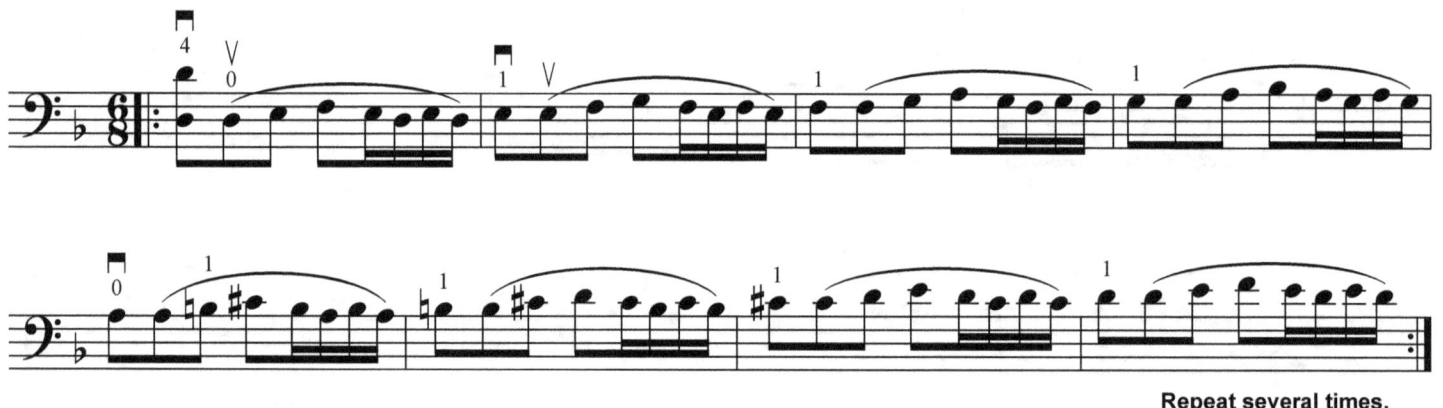

**Repeat several times, playing faster each time.**

### 72. Speed V: Measures 221-228

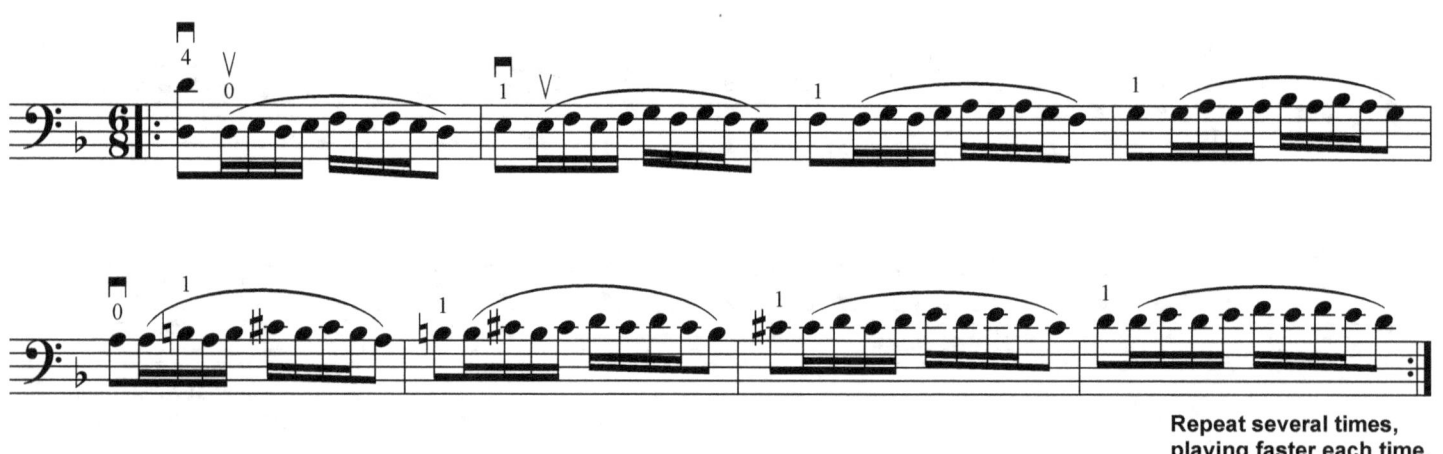

**Repeat several times, playing faster each time.**

### 73. Speed VI: Measures 221-228

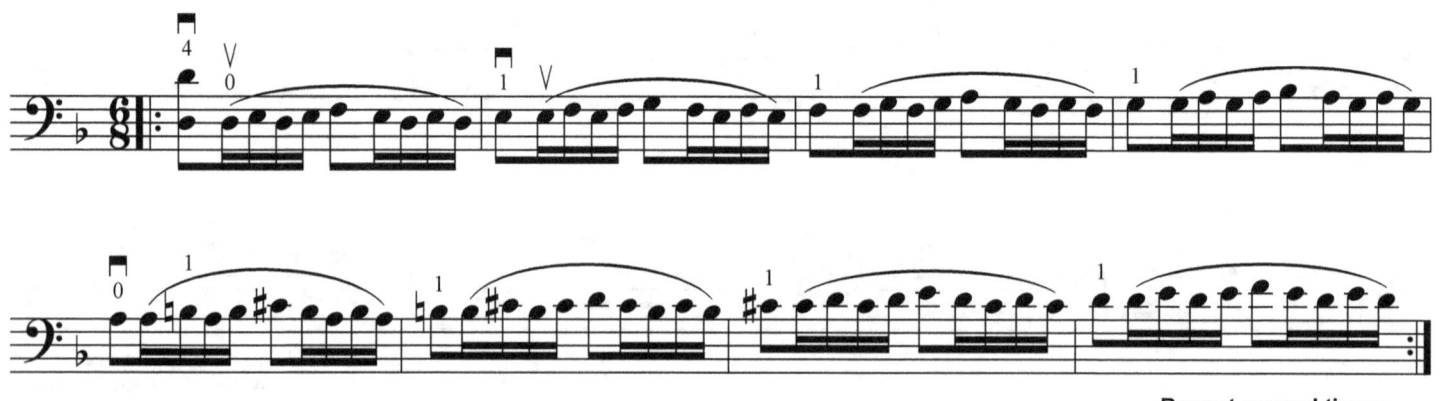

**Repeat several times, playing faster each time.**

This page is left blank for page turns.

56 — The Squire Tarantella for Cello Practice Edition - Piece with Study Notes

# Tarantella

W. H. Squire
edited by C. Harvey

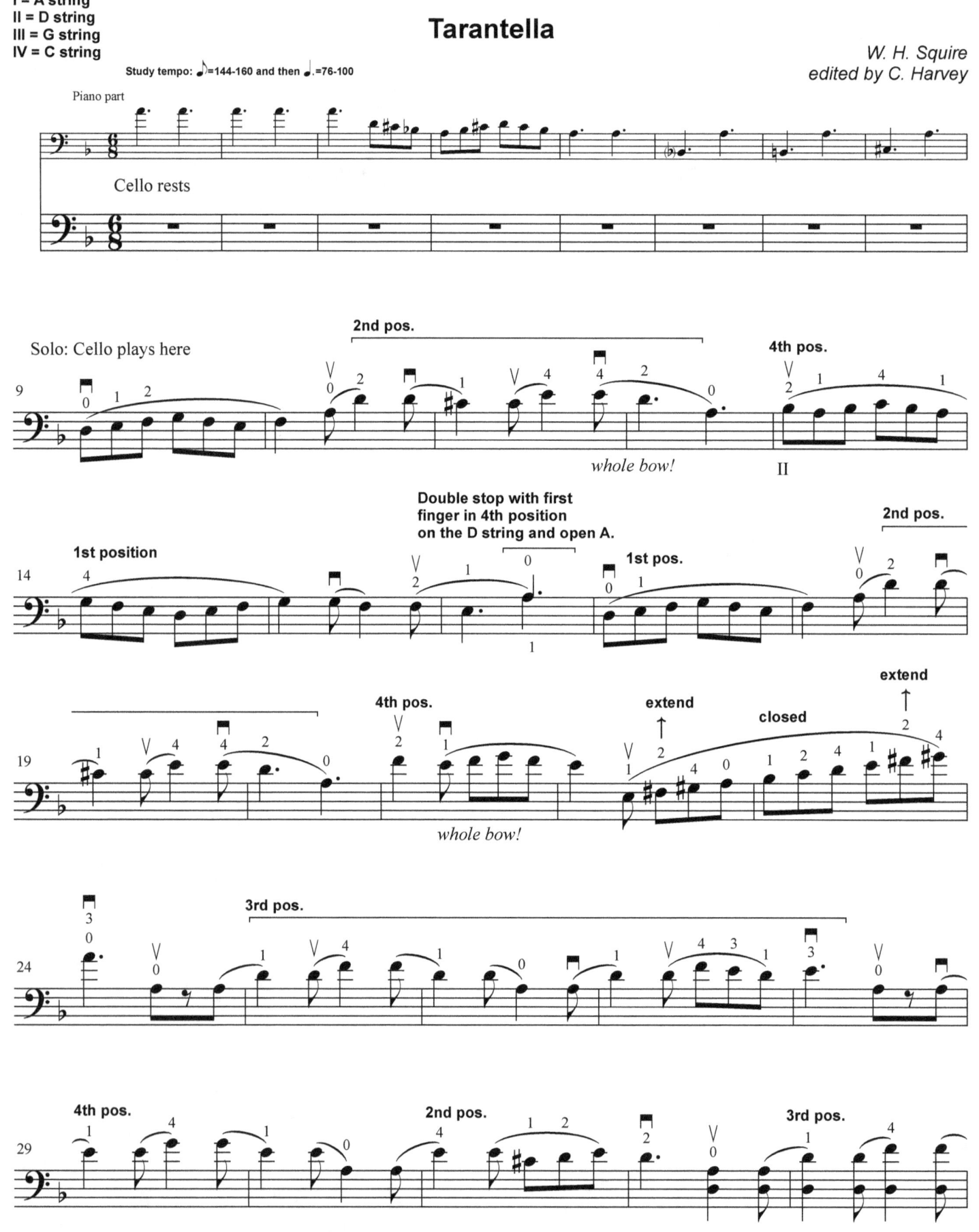

©2022 C. Harvey Publications®  All Rights Reserved.

The Squire Tarantella for Cello Practice Edition - Piece with Study Notes

57

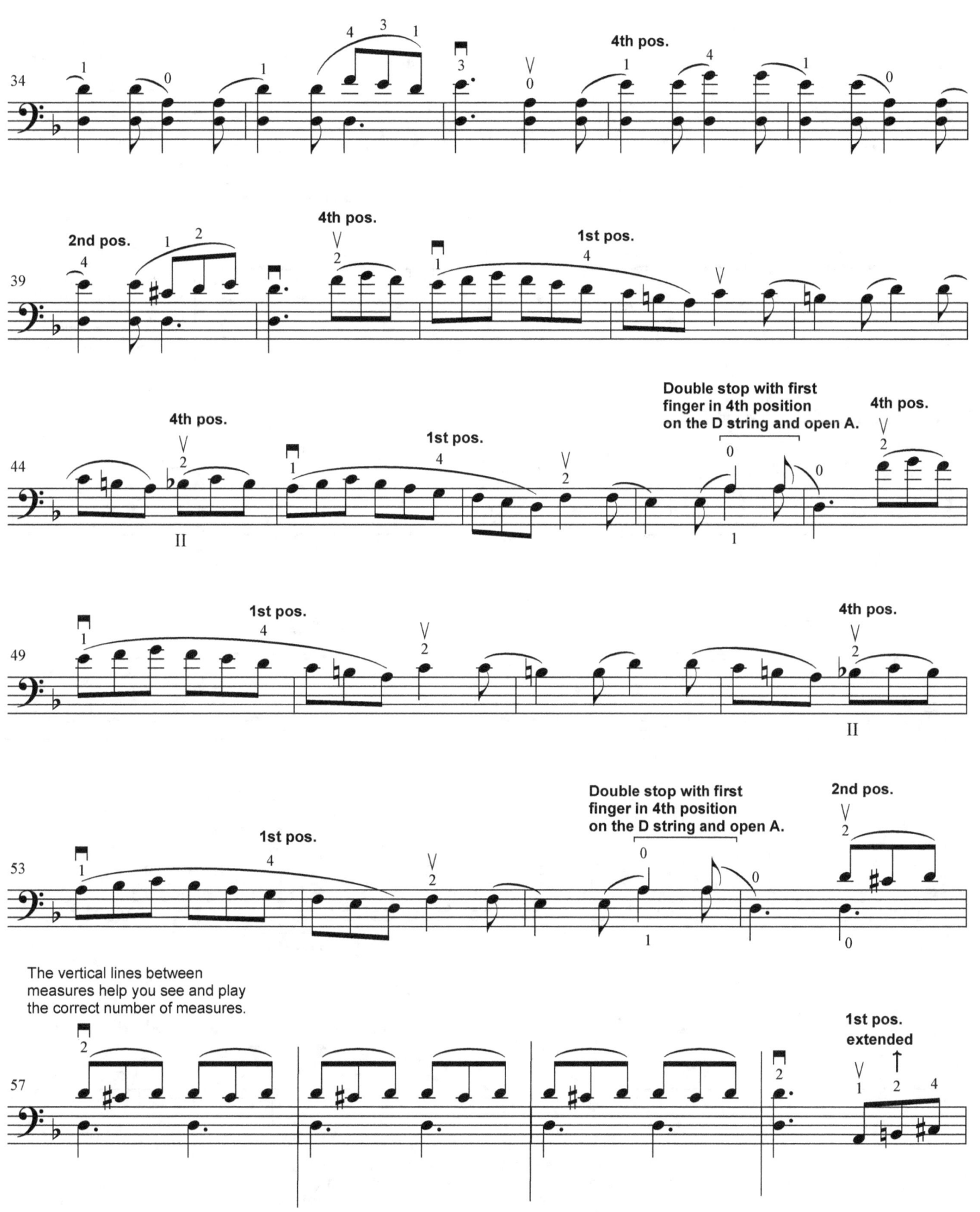

58

The Squire Tarantella for Cello Practice Edition - Piece with Study Notes

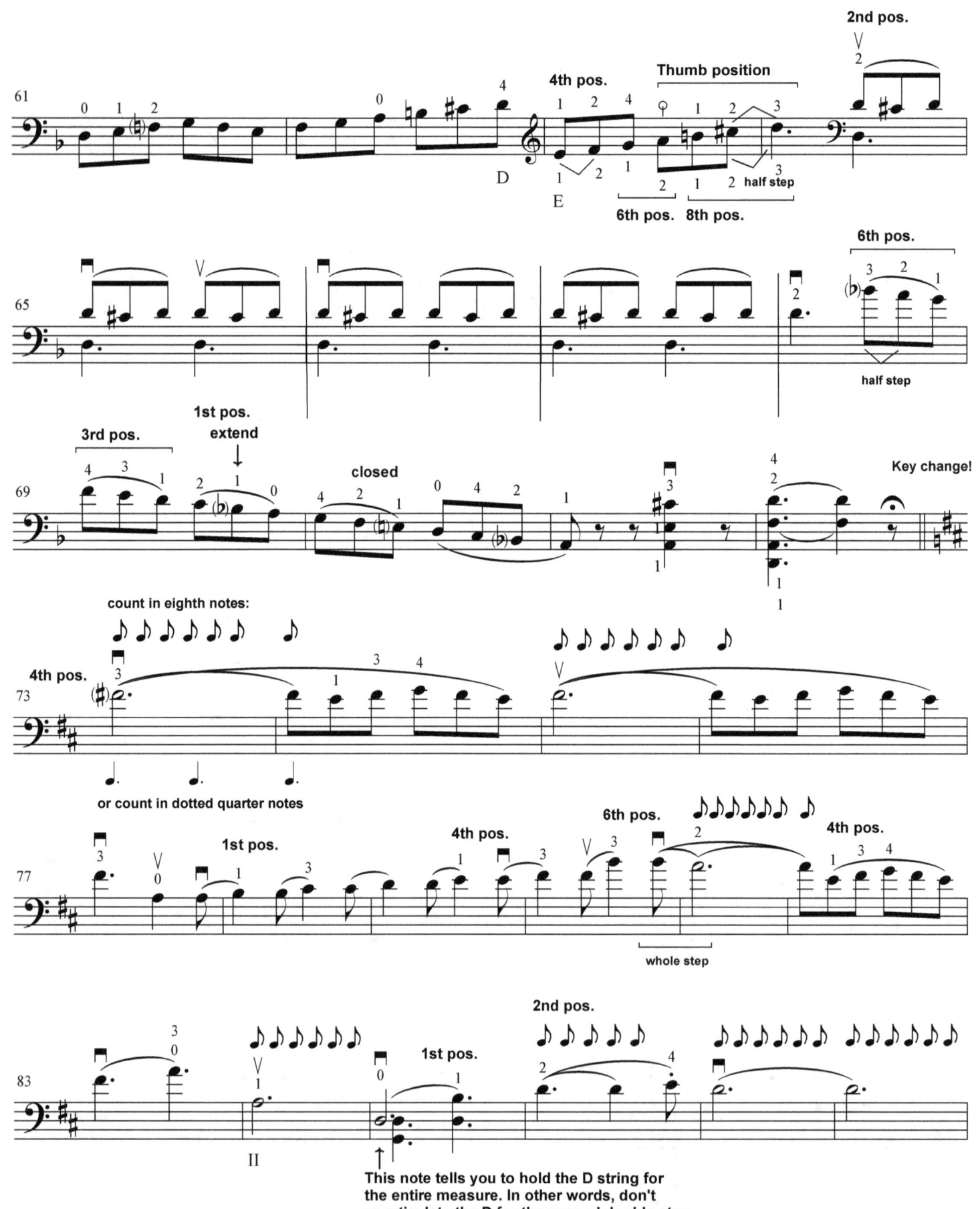

©2022 C. Harvey Publications®  All Rights Reserved.

The Squire Tarantella for Cello Practice Edition - Piece with Study Notes

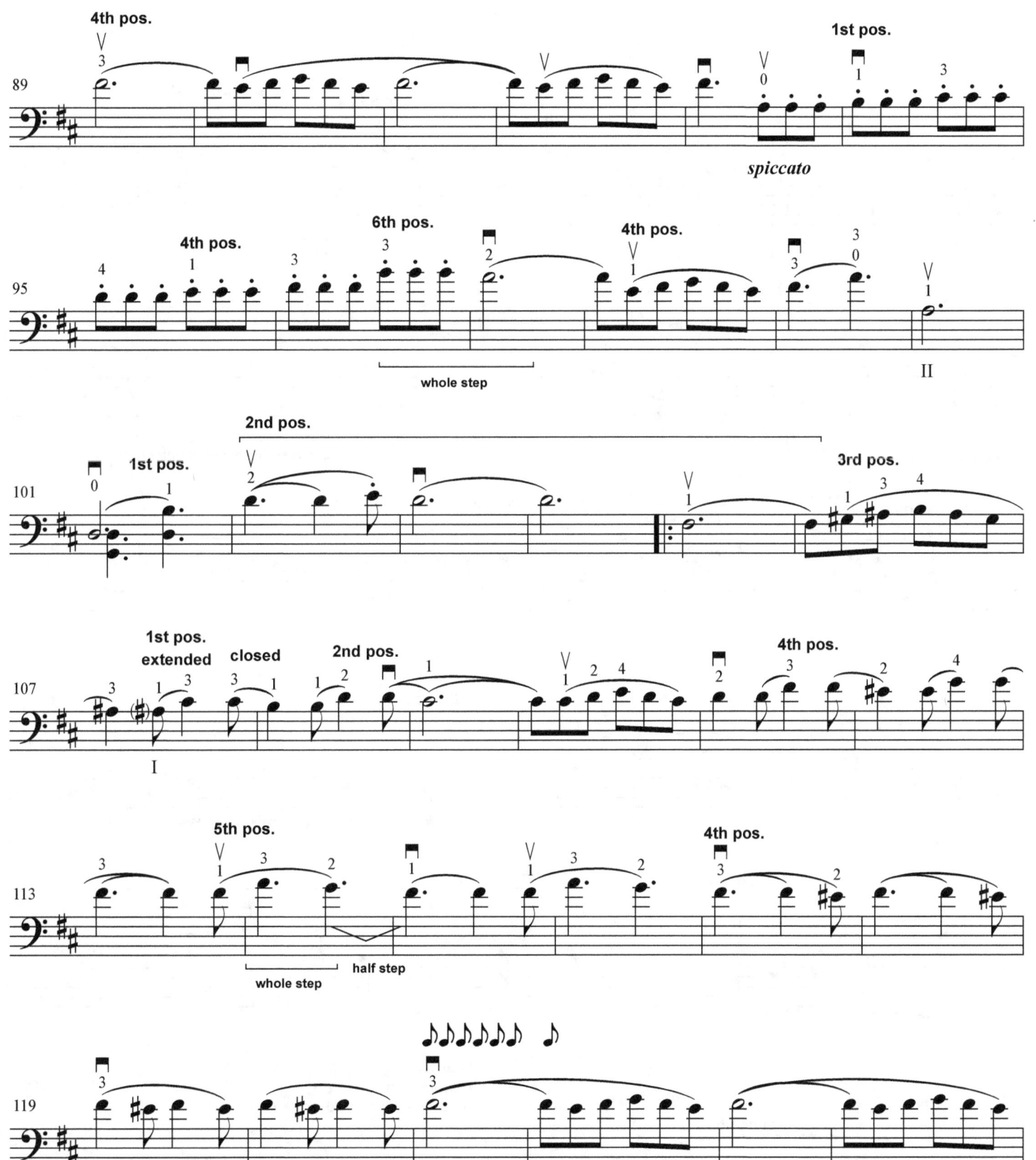

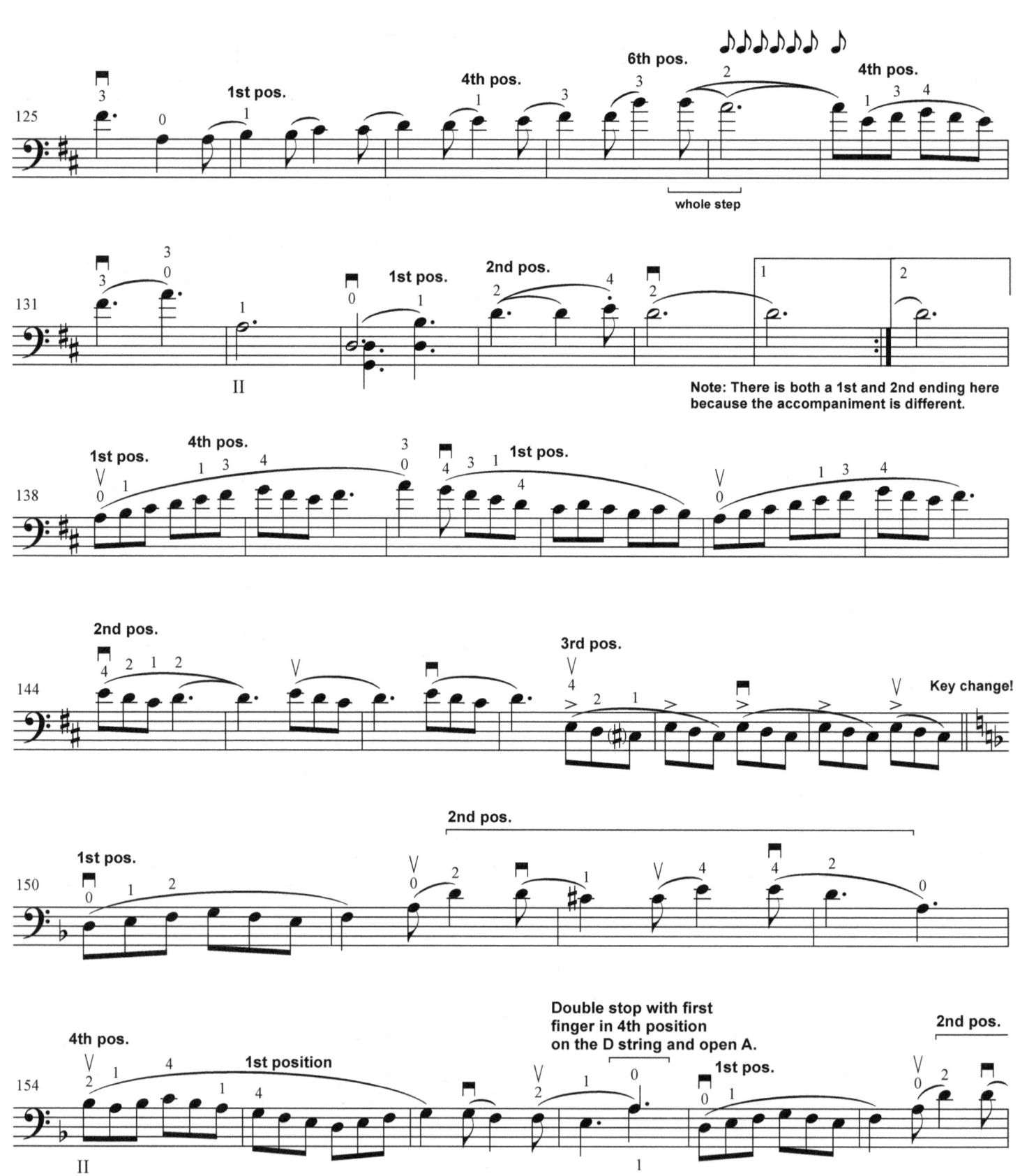

The Squire Tarantella for Cello Practice Edition - Piece with Study Notes

61

II

©2022 C. Harvey Publications®  All Rights Reserved.

62 — The Squire Tarantella for Cello Practice Edition - Piece with Study Notes

©2022 C. Harvey Publications®   All Rights Reserved.

The Squire Tarantella for Cello Practice Edition - Piece with Study Notes

This page is left blank for page turns.

The Squire Tarantella for Cello Practice Edition - Complete Piece  65

# Tarantella

Performance tempo: ♩.=104-144

W. H. Squire
edited by C. Harvey

Allegro con spirito

©2022 C. Harvey Publications®  All Rights Reserved.

The Squire Tarantella for Cello Practice Edition - Complete Piece

67

# Tarantella

**Allegro con spirito**

W. H. Squire, edited by C. Harvey
Duet by Myanna Harvey, based on W. H. Squire

The Squire Tarantella for Cello Practice Edition - Cello Duet
69

The Squire Tarantella for Cello Practice Edition - Cello Duet

The Squire Tarantella for Cello Practice Edition - Cello Duet

The Squire Tarantella for Cello Practice Edition - Cello Duet

The Squire Tarantella for Cello Practice Edition - Cello Two

75

Cello Two

# Tarantella

Duet part by Myanna Harvey
after W. H. Squire

©2022 C. Harvey Publications® All Rights Reserved.

The Squire Tarantella for Cello Practice Edition - Cello Two 77

# Tarantella

W. H. Squire
Edited by C. Harvey

The Squire Tarantella for Cello Practice Edition - Piano Accompaniment

80

The Squire Tarantella for Cello Practice Edition - Piano Accompaniment

82 — The Squire Tarantella for Cello Practice Edition - Piano Accompaniment

©2022 C. Harvey Publications® All Rights Reserved.

The Squire Tarantella for Cello Practice Edition - Piano Accompaniment

©2022 C. Harvey Publications®  All Rights Reserved.

# Cello Curriculum Segments
# When to Use the Tarantella in a Course of Study
## Step One

### Methods
- Learning the Cello, Books One (CHP282) and Two (CHP287)
- String Builder, Book One (published Belwin)
- Essential Elements for Cello, Book One (published Hal Leonard)
- Suzuki Book One (if using a modified Suzuki approach) (published Summy-Birchard)

### Exercises
- The Open-String Book for Cello (CHP182)
- Early Exercises for Cello (CHP183)
- Beginning Technique for Cello (CHP110)
- Double Stop Beginnings for Cello (CHP220)
- First Position Scale Studies for the Cello (CHP179)
- Playing in Keys for Cello (CHP242)
- Cello Stretching; Extended First Position (CHP243)

### Supplements and Etudes
- The Cello Etude System, Part 0 (CHP411) and Part 1A (CHP413)
- Cello Book One (CHP221)
- Playing the Cello, Book One (CHP300)

### Repertoire Books
- Stepping Stones for Cello (published Boosey & Hawkes)
- Waggon Wheels for Cello (published Boosey & Hawkes)
- Solo Time for Strings, Book One (published Alfred)
- String Festival Solos, Book One (published Belwin)

### Sonatas/Concertinos
- Reinagle Sonatina in G Major ((published Schott)
- Breval Concertino No. 4 in C Major, arr. Feuillard (published Delrieu)
- Schaffrath Sonata in G Major (published Schott)
- Matz Sonata da Camera (published Dominis Music)
- Breval Concertino No. 5 in D Major, arr. Feuillard (published Delrieu)

Note: Books published by C. Harvey Publications are noted with an item number (CHP101) and are available at www.charveypublications.com and/or www.learnstrings.com.

## Step Two: Early-Intermediate Level; Starting to Shift

### Methods
- Fourth Position for the Cello (CHP131) or Fourth Position Study Book for Cello (CHPD078)
- Second Position for the Cello (CHP114)
- Third Position for the Cello (CHP116)
- Suzuki Books Two and Three (if using a modified Suzuki approach) (published Summy-Birchard)

### Exercises
- Finger Exercises for Cello, Book One (CHP101)
- Open-String Bow Workouts for Cello, Book One (CHP351)

### Supplements and Etudes
- Squire Twelve Easy Exercises (published Stainer and Bell)
- Dotzauer 113 Studies, Book One (published International)
- Flying Fiddle Duets for Two Cellos, Book One (CHP272)
- Playing the Cello, Book Two (CHP326)

### Repertoire Books
- Solo Time for Strings, Book Two (published Alfred)
- String Festival Solos, Book Two (published Belwin)
- Pejtsik Violoncello Music for Beginners, Vol. 3, (published EMB)

### Sonatas/Concertinos (in approximate order of study)
- Breval Sonata in C Major
- Marcello Sonata in E Minor (published International)

Note: Books published by C. Harvey Publications are noted with an item number (CHP101) and are available at www.charveypublications.com and/or www.learnstrings.com.

©2022 C. Harvey Publications® All Rights Reserved.

# Step Three: Intermediate Level; Becoming Fluent in the Lower and Neck Positions

## Methods
- Fifth Position for the Cello (CHP198)
- Suzuki Books Three, Four (if using a modified Suzuki approach) (published Summy-Birchard)
- Francesconi Scuola Pratica Del Violoncello (published Suvini Zerboni)

## Exercises
- Serial Shifting for the Cello (CHP106)
- Finger Exercises for Cello, Book Two (CHP130)
- Double Stop Etudes for the Cello (CHP202)

## Scales
- The Two Octaves Book for Cello (CHP122)

## Supplements and Etudes
- Schroeder 170 Foundation Studies, Vol. 1 (published Carl Fischer)
- Flying Fiddle Duets for Two Cellos, Book Two (CHP309)

## Short Pieces
- Squire Bourree (published Carl Fischer)
- **Squire Tarantella (this book)**

## Bach
- The Bach Cello Suite No. 1 Study Book (CHP332)

## Sonatas/Concertos (in approximate order of study)
- Romberg Sonata in E Minor (this book)
- Romberg Sonata in C Major Study Book (CHP348)
- Goltermann Concerto No. 4 Study Book for Cello (CHP364)

Note: Books published by C. Harvey Publications are noted with an item number (CHP101) and are available at www.charveypublications.com and/or www.learnstrings.com, as well as where you purchased this book.

©2022 C. Harvey Publications®  All Rights Reserved.

# Step Four: Late-Intermediate Level; Adding Tenor Clef and the Higher Positions

## Methods
- De'ak Modern Method for the Cello, Book Two (published Presser)
- Tenor Clef for the Cello (CHP109)
- Suzuki Book Five (if using a modified Suzuki approach) (published Summy-Birchard)

## Exercises
- The Shifting Book for Cello, Part One (CHP171) and Part Two (CHP172)
- Shifting in Keys for Cello, Book One (CHP244)
- Double Stop Shifting for Cello (CHP219)
- Octave Shifts for the Cello, Book One (CHP104)
- Finger Exercises for Cello, Book Three (CHP142)

## Scales
- Learning Three-Octave Scales on the Cello (CHP356)
- The C Major Scale Book for Cello (CHP117)
- Arpeggio Studies in Two Octaves for Cello (CHP155)

## Supplements and Etudes
- Feuillard 60 Etudes for the Young Cellist (published Delrieu)
- Schroeder 170 Foundation Studies, Vol. 2 (published Carl Fischer)
- Lee 40 Melodic and Progressive Etudes, Vol. 1 (Published Schirmer)

## Short Pieces
- Squire Danse Rustique (published Carl Fischer)
- Saint-Saens The Swan Study Book (CHP346)
- Saint-Saens Allegro Appassionato (published Carl Fischer)
- Faure Elegie Study Book (CHP319)

## Bach
- Bach Cello Suites No. 2,3 (published Barenreiter as 6 Suites for Solo Violoncello)

## Sonatas/Concertos (in approximate order of study)
- Klengel Concertino in C Major (published International)
- Romberg Sonata in G Major, Op. 43, No. 3 (published International)

Note: Books published by C. Harvey Publications are noted with an item number (CHP101) and are available at www.charveypublications.com and/or www.learnstrings.com.

©2022 C. Harvey Publications®  All Rights Reserved.

# Also Available from C. Harvey Publications

## The Romberg Sonata in C Major Study Book for Cello
## CHP348

- Exercises are included to teach you every measure.
- Essential cello technique is distilled and presented.
- The complete cello part to the Sonata is included.
- Master the Sonata that comes after the Romberg Sonata in E Minor!

www.charveypublications.com - print books
www.learnstrings.com - downloadable books

©2022 C. Harvey Publications®  All Rights Reserved.

# You Might Also Like:

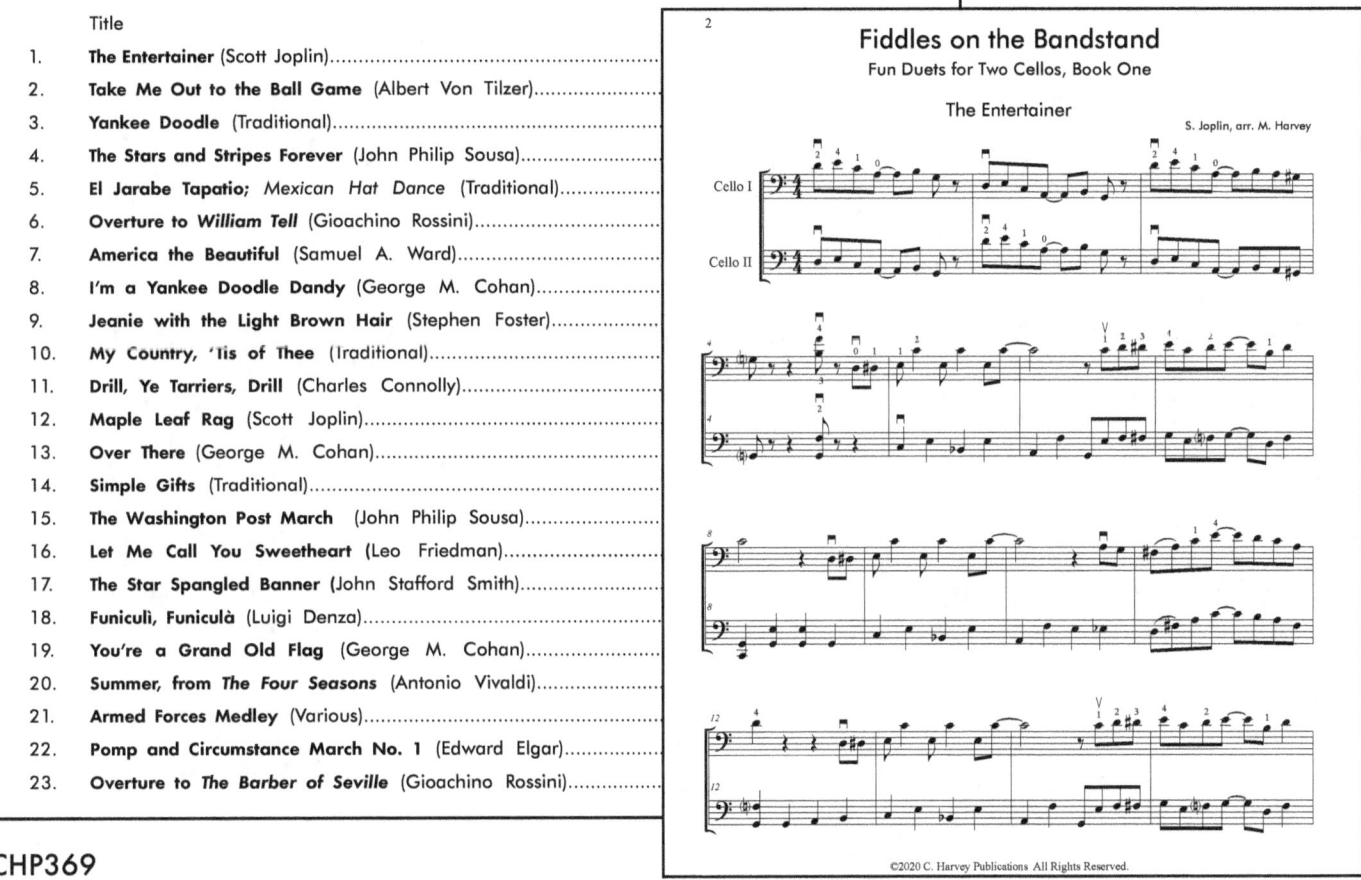

**Fiddles on the Bandstand: Fun Duets for Two Cellos, Book One**

all duets arranged by Myanna Harvey

Table of Contents

| # | Title |
|---|---|
| 1. | **The Entertainer** (Scott Joplin) |
| 2. | **Take Me Out to the Ball Game** (Albert Von Tilzer) |
| 3. | **Yankee Doodle** (Traditional) |
| 4. | **The Stars and Stripes Forever** (John Philip Sousa) |
| 5. | **El Jarabe Tapatio;** *Mexican Hat Dance* (Traditional) |
| 6. | **Overture to** *William Tell* (Gioachino Rossini) |
| 7. | **America the Beautiful** (Samuel A. Ward) |
| 8. | **I'm a Yankee Doodle Dandy** (George M. Cohan) |
| 9. | **Jeanie with the Light Brown Hair** (Stephen Foster) |
| 10. | **My Country, 'Tis of Thee** (Traditional) |
| 11. | **Drill, Ye Tarriers, Drill** (Charles Connolly) |
| 12. | **Maple Leaf Rag** (Scott Joplin) |
| 13. | **Over There** (George M. Cohan) |
| 14. | **Simple Gifts** (Traditional) |
| 15. | **The Washington Post March** (John Philip Sousa) |
| 16. | **Let Me Call You Sweetheart** (Leo Friedman) |
| 17. | **The Star Spangled Banner** (John Stafford Smith) |
| 18. | **Funiculì, Funiculà** (Luigi Denza) |
| 19. | **You're a Grand Old Flag** (George M. Cohan) |
| 20. | **Summer, from** *The Four Seasons* (Antonio Vivaldi) |
| 21. | **Armed Forces Medley** (Various) |
| 22. | **Pomp and Circumstance March No. 1** (Edward Elgar) |
| 23. | **Overture to** *The Barber of Seville* (Gioachino Rossini) |

CHP369

www.charveypublications.com

Take a journey to a simpler time when lawn chairs and blankets would be out under the stars and music would waft out from under the eaves of the wooden bandstand.

These are the tunes that got our feet moving, made us smile, and brought us together. Now, with these cello duets, you can bring the toe-tapping, exuberant joy to others and remind us all that through highs and lows, music can be something we share to keep our spirits up and build community.

From Scott Joplin to John Philip Sousa, these cello duets will invite you up on the bandstand, out for a gig, or out on your lawn to play your heart out! Know any violinists or violists? You can pick up a copy of the violin or viola book and play with those instruments as well; the cello book is fully compatible with the violin and viola books.

This cello book is in first through fourth positions, is entirely in bass clef, and is at an intermediate level.

©2022 C. Harvey Publications® All Rights Reserved.

www.ingramcontent.com/pod-product-compliance
Lightning Source LLC
Chambersburg PA
CBHW081406070526
44583CB00020B/2691